"As someone who has been responsible for the printing of more than 100 million books, I am very concerned about the effects of that on the environment. I am glad there is a book addressing the issue with solid ideas that we can all implement. I hope everyone in publishing reads this book."

~ Jack Canfield,
Co-author, Chicken Soup for the Soul® series

"It's effortless ease to save our planet and get 'green'.
It's the only home we've got.
Read this great guide and make your book 'green'."

~ Mark Victor Hansen,
Co-creator, Chicken Soup for the Soul® series

"This brilliant little book teaches you how to make more green by making your book 'green

~ Robert G. Allen,
Best-selling author of
Multiple Streams of Income
and Co-founder of Bookwise.com

The Green Guide Girls:
Guide to Book Publishing

Cindy Katz
&
Jennifer S. Wilkov

KNOW WHAT TO DO.

Published by E.S.P. Press Corp.
189 Montague Street, Ste 900, Brooklyn, NY 11201, USA

The Green Guide Girls: Guide to Book Publishing
by Cindy Katz & Jennifer S. Wilkov
Copyright © 2007 E.S.P. Press Corp.

All Rights Reserved.

Cover design: YAY! Design/Text design: Craig P. Cardone

Interior Printed and Book Manufactured in Michigan by Thomson-Shore, Inc.
Cover Printed in Missouri by Pinnacle Press, Inc.

First printing May 2007

ISBN 0-9777347-6-5

Additional copies of this book may be purchased at a discount for educational, business, or sales promotional use by contacting the publisher through info@GreenGuideGirls.com

Visit www.GreenGuideGirls.com and www.GetMyESPPress.com

This book is dedicated to you, yes, you, the reader …

… And to all the kids, boys and girls, with pigtails or not,
grown people and kids at heart,
who know that to find the information to get what you want,
you just have to ASK …

"How do we make THAT 'green'?"™

Contents

FOREWORD

Tyson Miller, Director, Green Press Initiative

Books add a tremendous value to advancing the development and evolution of our shared society. As an author, your voice is an important part of the evolving story of balance, stewardship, and responsibility. There is a spectrum of steps that you can take—from simply asking questions and encouraging your publisher to join their peer companies in making meaningful changes to contractually requiring that your book be on paper produced to the best practices in environmental management. I know that this resource guide will help you along the way!

A handful of notable authors including Alice Walker and Barbara Kingsolver require that their books be printed on paper with high levels of recycled fiber. Now, it is easier than ever with over sixty environmentally responsible book papers available and stocked by over twenty book printers. The book industry is in the midst of a transformation—with over 140 publishers with environmental policies in place.

Despite the valuable contribution of book publishing, the current book paper production and consumption cycle, as with many industries, can still be improved in a manner which benefits the common good. Many publishers, paper mills, printers, authors, and others have been and will continue to drive this transformation.

The world of responsible paper and production has many layers to it and includes phrases like post-consumer recycled fiber, Carbon Neutral, Forest Stewardship Council or FSC, Processed Chlorine Free and a range of other technical sounding terms. Yet there is still need for continued progress as some publishers haven't quite yet integrated the principles of social and environmental stewardship into the way in which they produce books.

This resource guide will help you and your publisher to navigate these waters.

It is an easier journey than one might think!

Kind wishes,

Tyson Miller
Director of the Green Press Initiative

An Eco-Audit is most likely available for whichever parts of your book you choose to make "green". Ask your publisher, book manufacturer, printer or consultant if they can assist you by providing this valuable insight for you for your book.

This Eco-Audit is provided by
Thomson-Shore, Inc.
based on the procedures from the
Green Press Initiative.

This audit is for the interior of our book which was manufactured by Thomson-Shore, Inc.

green press INITIATIVE

E.S.P. Press Corp. is committed to preserving ancient forests and natural resources. We elected to print *The Green Guide Girls: Guide to Book Publishing* on 100% post consumer recycled paper, processed chlorine free. As a result, for this printing, we have saved:

7.7 Trees (40' tall and 6-8" diameter)
3,282.7 Gallons of Wastewater
1,320.2 Kilowatt Hours of Electricity
361.8 Pounds of Solid Waste
710.9 Pounds of Greenhouse Gases

E.S.P. Press Corp. made this paper choice because our printer, Thomson-Shore, Inc., is a member of Green Press Initiative, a nonprofit program dedicated to supporting authors, publishers, and suppliers in their efforts to reduce their use of fiber obtained from endangered forests.

For more information, visit www.greenpressinitiative.org

An Eco-Audit is most likely available for whichever parts of your book you choose to make "green". Ask your publisher, book manufacturer, printer or consultant if they can assist you by providing this valuable insight for you for your book.

This Eco-Audit is provided by
New Leaf Paper
based on their proprietary procedures.

This audit is for the cover materials of our book which was manufactured by Pinnacle Press, Inc.

NEW LEAF PAPER®
ENVIRONMENTAL BENEFITS STATEMENT
of using post-consumer waste fiber vs. virgin fiber

Green Guide Girls saved the following resources by using New Leaf Sakura 100, manufactured with Green-e® certified renewable energy, 100% post-consumer waste, and processed chlorine free.

trees	water	energy	solid waste	greenhouse gases
4 fully grown	1,127 gallons	2 million Btu	163 pounds	316 pounds

Calculations based on research by Environmental Defense and other members of the Paper Task Force.

©2007 New Leaf Paper   www.newleafpaper.com

The Green Guide Girls™ Combined Eco-Audit

We were curious about how ALL of the "green" choices we made during the process of publishing *The Green Guide Girls: Guide to Book Publishing* added up. So we took it upon ourselves to take the numbers from the Green Press Initiative Eco-Audit of the interior pages and add them with the New Leaf Paper Eco-Audit of the cover materials to determine our own combined Eco-Audit for our book. We determined on our own by using simple math that we have saved the following resources.

Trees ~ 11.7 fully grown
Water ~ 4409.7 gallons of wastewater
Electricity ~ 1906.3 Kilowatt hours
Solid waste ~ 524.8 pounds
Greenhouse gases ~ 1026.9 pounds

INTRODUCTION

S ome people view the subject of "green" book publishing as a serious matter. While we agree that it is "serious", we feel that a lighter approach creates an atmosphere filled with joy, purpose and most of all—collaboration. We, the Green Guide Girls™, welcome you to join us in a warm and friendly classroom filled with pigtails and raised hands where we can all learn together ~ "How do we make THAT 'green'?"™

When people think about the book publishing industry, often times their thoughts turn to authors they love, books they enjoy, sections of the bookstore they like to browse in, and perhaps of one day becoming an author themselves. Eventually, some of them follow their dream and do join the ranks of the best-selling award winning author community. We know that some of you who are reading this book are already in this elite group—with the credit of "author" attached to your name.

As the Green Guide Girls™, our purpose is to help people just like you in every stage of your writing and publishing career. You see, we want to raise your awareness of the opportunity that you have to make a conscious choice about how you want to produce your book. There is a moment during this process in which your decision impacts the health and wealth of the environment and the world around us. This book provides you with the information, knowledge and resources to support your educated decision to make your book "green". When we have furnished this for you, we have fulfilled our mission in a joyful, light and fun way. We create a world of collaboration to tap into so you can make the best decision that is right for you. It is then up to you to choose how "green" you want your book to be.

Everyone Can Be An Author

We believe that everyone has the heart of an author and the mind for writing. Funny, that is how we met ~ when we joined the elite educational community of two of our beloved best-selling authors, Mark Victor Hansen and Robert G. Allen. "Community" is a great experience. You just never know who you are going to meet.

We met and connected through the group meetings during the year. One of those meetings was during Book Expo America where we really got a chance to learn more about each other and how we were each impacting the book industry on our own.

Jennifer is a best-selling award winning author. She is the creative mind and big heart behind the *Dating Your Money* series. She loves being an author and has a lot to share and teach. She is also a publisher and book consultant through her company, E.S.P. Press Corp. Publishing is one of her deepest passions. She loves to help others enjoy the beautiful gift of being an author and sharing and expressing themselves through their books. As a consultant, Jennifer feels blessed with the enormous privilege of guiding select authors through the process of understanding publishing and promoting their book and message—so it becomes a business that can support their lives, families and dreams.

Cindy is the founder of Plant a Tree USA™, where she excites and educates every industry and individual about creating a healthy Mother Earth, with a passion. As a speaker and businesswoman, she teaches and encourages audiences of all sizes about the value of reforestation, the planting of more and more (and more) trees. Cindy offers her services as a resource for companies to learn how to save money and make money by being "green". She leads the Plant a Tree USA™ (PATUSA) team in creating Environmentally Conscious Business Growth™ (ECBG) techniques and assists clients with putting these into practice. Cindy also creates programs that build win-win relationships with authors, artists, individuals, organizations, and businesses to incorporate tree plantings in their daily pursuits.

Cindy introduced Jennifer to the Author Save World™ program that she offers to publishers and authors through Plant a Tree USA™. Jennifer was intrigued and asked to learn more about it. Eventually, Jennifer and her publishing company, E.S.P. Press Corp., became one of the early adopters to join Cindy in this great effort to educate others about the value of planting and saving trees while publishing more books.

In early 2007, Cindy came to one of Jennifer's famous "Let Your Life Speak" publishing workshops and sparked an idea for a book during the ninety minute interactive workshop. She realized that she had this great program, Author Save World™, but did not have a book of her own. Cindy knew she could be an author. After the workshop, she understood that she did have a book to write — many of them.

Shortly after the workshop, she approached Jennifer with an idea about writing a book to educate authors in a fun and simple way about all the resources available to make their books using environmentally friendly practices. Then she said, "I want you to write this with me." Jennifer reflected on this invitation to teach authors and publishers about this approach to determine if it was right for her. When Jennifer agreed ~ the Green Guide Girls™ were born.

We believe that everybody can be an author.

Everybody Can Build a Team

As an author, you recognize that no one completes a book project alone. It takes a team to build and produce a book. If you are working with a partner, the building blocks start here.

So we began with ourselves. We had to figure out how our similar interests would work together. Cindy is green in heart and mind. She has always followed her deep interest in eco-friendly practices; however, she found it somewhat of a challenge to find trusted resources that could help her put her beliefs into practice. Jennifer developed her interest in ecologically sound practices as she continued to be exposed to "green-friendly" options that she did not know were available.

Cindy's strength is her interest in asking questions and forming great relationships with colleagues in every industry and organization she speaks with. Jennifer's strength is leading and attracting dynamic championship teams to bring the message of the author to the marketplace through a congruent, simple approach. When we got together, our greatest combined strength was building alliances and friendships. We put on our pigtails as the Green Guide Girls™ and began to think about who we needed to talk with so we could fill our book with lots of valuable information that was easy to understand and implement.

So we went to the top and began building our team. Before we knew it, we had attracted eight of the greatest minds from the "green" publishing world to our project. We began with one person who suggested the next person and so on. We kept asking who each person thought we should talk with next. Because we asked, we received immediate assistance. Before we knew it, we had built a powerful team of eight experts across every area of the "green" book publishing industry. From printers to book manufacturers, suppliers and publishers, we created our advisory group that we affectionately dubbed our "Collective Wisdom Team™."

We believe that anyone can build a team for any project when the individual is willing to become vulnerable, allow others to know that you don't know, and ask for the guidance and assistance you need.

Everyone Can Produce A Book

From the very beginning of the process as you pick your cover and decide if your book will be a hardcover or paperback, you as an author have lots of choices to make. Then the paper, ink and cover materials must be thoughtfully chosen to go with your subject matter.

Many authors approach their publisher and publishing team with the thought that someone at the company is going to want to take their book manuscript, give them a big check for it as an advance, and then receive a royalty payment while they write the next book.

For some, this may feel similar to believing in the myth of the tooth fairy or Santa Claus. Yet, for many, this dream does become a reality. Ideas, thoughts, messages and information are constantly provided through the amazing book production process, whether authors choose to print on paper or make an e-book.

We examined the book publishing process and talked about it in depth. We realized that no one was really talking about how the book gets produced. It was all about how to get a publisher to buy your manuscript from you and make you a star.

We knew there was so much more to book publishing, so we explored and asked our amazing Collective Wisdom Team™, "How do they do THAT?" Everyone welcomed our "pigtails" approach to the industry so we could learn from the experts how much consideration goes into producing a book. We found the love each person had for books resonated with our goal of bringing an intelligent, informative book to the marketplace.

We believe that everyone can produce their book and enjoy learning about the components of the process in a simple and friendly way.

Everybody Can Be "Green"

As we thought about life, we realized that it was a giant classroom. Our shared interest in the environment, nature and the outdoors was the spark that brought us together and turned our inquiries to the "green" world of book publishing. We decided to have fun with our project, raise our hands, and ask our simple question, "How do we make THAT 'green'?"™

Lo and behold, resources began pouring in to help us understand and explore the world of "green" book publishing. We found that our Collective Wisdom Team™ offered more than one hundred years of combined experience in the "green" publishing industry. They have led the evolution of "green" book publishing processes and environmentally sound approaches to making any book ecologically-friendly.

What we learned was that when authors and publishers ask, the industry responds to their needs and desires to produce their books with the least impact on the planet. This was important to authors and industry professionals alike. In some cases, their small decisions and steadfast requests to the printers and book manufacturers became the catalyst that revolutionized the "green" book publishing industry.

We have been amazed to learn from such valuable experiences. We have been blessed with a passionate group of people who, like us, support the idea of a sound approach to publishing using the mind, body, spirit and earth as assets.

We all agree ~ everybody can make their book "green". We are going to show you how in this simple, easy to read guidebook. We will help you to understand your options during every step of the publishing process. It is a fact: You make a difference in the way publishing books continues to support or destroy the planet.

Everybody Can Save the Planet In a Moment By Just Asking...

Without the author, the publishing world does not exist. There would be no one to serve. The author has to bring forth their ideas in order for the book industry to survive and thrive.

As the Green Guide Girls™, we know that it is in that one moment of decision, that one breath when you say to your publisher, book manufacturer, printer and book consultant, "Would you like to publish my book?" that everything begins. We also know that in that same breath, there is one question that has the power to transform the world and the industry as we know it.

We encourage you to ask, "How do we make THAT book 'green'?"™

If you are not confident about how to do this, this guidebook will give you all the tools, insights, resources and information you need to strike up this conversation with your publishing team and printer.

In one moment, the whole planet has the opportunity to benefit from your book. From the paper chosen to print it on to the ink on your page, your decision to ask this simple question holds the key to the sustainable future of Planet Earth.

We know that everybody can save the planet in a moment by just asking.

Yes, two girls in pigtails really do make this stuff about being "green" easy to understand and take the mystery out of the whole process. The Green Guide Girls™ have done the work and brought the top green experts in the publishing world to you. We asked the questions...Now you get the guide. We tell you what and where the resources are—and how to get to them—to support your educated decisions about how "green" you want your book to be.

It is our honor, privilege and mission to assist you in understanding the many options available and the amazing benefits everyone receives when you choose to make your book "green".

Thank you from the bottom of our little Green Guide Girl™ hearts for the opportunity to share this book with you.

Be well and prosper green.

Warmly with respect and gratitude,

Cindy Katz   Jennifer S. Wilkov

The Green Guide Girls™

HOW TO USE THIS BOOK

Thank you for choosing to take the Green Guide Girls™ along with you on your amazing journey as an author and publisher. We know that taking it with you is the key to your success in "green" book publishing. It will open doors and dialogues with the friendly resources in the industry to help you make your book using ecologically sound practices.

This book has been designed for you as a simple guide—sort of like a "cheat sheet"—to understand what "green" book publishing is and the spectrum of choices available to you for making your book environmentally friendly.

We have asked the leaders in the "green" book publishing industry to help us educate and inform you of how your production choices impact us all. They helped us define what "green" book publishing is in their own words. They showed us the various options for making your book a little bit "green" or "green" from cover to cover. Read their visions for the future of ecologically sound book publishing practices. See how every publisher, book manufacturer, printer and book consultant can promote the benefits of "green" book publishing to their clients and authors through their every day business practices.

As the Green Guide Girls™, we have consolidated the information and insights we have learned from our trusted Collective Wisdom Team™. At the end of each chapter you will find tips from us: ESP Tips™ — Environmentally Sound Principles — and PAT Tips™ — Please Act Today action steps — that inspire and inform you to make it easy to talk with your publishing team and printer.

In the back of the book is a brief glossary that will assist you with understanding those words that may be new to you in the "green" book publishing world.

We have also included a list of resources so it is easy to find someone to help you. Whether you enlist the assistance of our Collective Wisdom Team™ or any company in the Resource section, everyone is ready and willing to help you with your "green" book publishing endeavor.

Whether you are writing and publishing your first book or if you are a seasoned author who wants to learn more about "green" book publishing options, we want you to be informed. We want you to know you have a choice. We want you to become aware of the opportunity you have to make a big difference in our world one page at a time — by understanding the value of making your book "green".

Get inspired by our Collective Wisdom Team™ and appreciate them with us. Your children and your children's children will someday reap the benefit of being able to look at a clear stream or a lush green forest because you took the time to talk with those who could assist you with making your book "green".

May this book be a blessing to you and those you love.

Be well and prosper green.

Warmly with respect and gratitude,

Cindy Katz   Jennifer S. Wilkov

The Green Guide Girls™

We ask the question:
"How do you make THAT 'green'?"™

Our mission: Through quick information and simple steps, we help people learn that it's easy to make anything "green".

www.greenguidegirls.com

CHAPTER : 1

Yes!

You Can Make Your Book "Green"!

Book publishing is both an art and science. Makin' it "green" is a phrase mentioned by many authors, publishers and printers throughout the industry.

Defining "green" book publishing could be a daunting task. We decided to ask our trusted Collective Wisdom Team™ to help us with providing this for you so we can elaborate about how it is done and the resources available to you in the rest of this book.

You see, "green" book publishing efforts have been around for more than thirty years. So if this is a new concept that you have become interested in or if you have been publishing your work for years, we would like to offer you a brief perspective of how far "green" book publishing has come in the past several years.

"Green" Book Publishing and What It Is All About

When you look up the definition of "green" in the Merriam-Webster dictionary, you will find references to, "concerned with or supporting environmentalism" and "tending to preserve environmental quality (as by being recyclable, biodegradable, or nonpolluting)."

When this is applied to the book publishing industry, the focus turns to the "environmental quality" and preservation of our natural resources.

Here is what some of the industry leaders in the world of "green" book publishing told us when we asked them to define this term:

"'Green' publishing, to me, means being environmentally sound. That word goes back to the mid-80's. In fact, I think I may have coined it one day when somebody said, 'Well, are you environmentally safe?' I thought about it a little bit and said, 'We really don't know that much about all of the things that go on in our environment, including in our coating and chemicals, so a better word would be 'environmentally sound'.' By saying 'environmentally sound' I mean using products that to the best of our knowledge do not harm our people or our environment — also part of this is to recycle and reuse as many of the byproducts that you generate through the book publishing processes, whether it be for something that you can continue to use in your own operation or something that is recycled or used in a different operation by someone else."

~ Stephen F. Quill,
Chairman – Ecological Fibers, Inc.

"'Green' publishing to me would be as if we are isolating publishing as an industry, looking at it as we do any other industry. You simply look at those places in an operation that performs publishing, including what are you doing and consider how you could, as a publisher, do something differently to create a sustainable planet for future generations. What comes instantly to mind would be: when publishing a book, rather than printing that book on virgin paper that uses forest resources, you can choose to publish on paper that is post-consumer recycled, made of old paper. It could be 100% post-consumer recycled paper printed with soy inks. This recycled paper is as clean and white as virgin paper, using only waste paper fibers as a resource. Even in something so simple as the fact that it takes lighting and electricity to run a publishing press or an operation, energy-efficient compact fluorescent bulbs can be used to light offices, plant facilities and workroom areas. A company could utilize renewable energy as a source for powering the plant that produces the book — to turn on the lights and run the facility that publishes the book. There are many ways to be 'green' – the paper, the books that get delivered in trucks. Think about it: are the trucks 'green'? Are they fuel efficient? Do they run on bio diesel? Are they possibly available in hybrid-drive technology? Additionally, are the administration offices, supporting the plant operations, using recycled-content office supplies and Energy Star office equipment? So there are a lot of different areas that 'green' publishing could be a reality and assist in moving us toward a planet that is more sustainable."

~ *Tom Kemper,*
CEO & Founder, Dolphin Blue

"In 'green' publishing, most people think of it as just a paper, and obviously that is the biggest focus that everybody has. We consider paper to be the medium for the message. When individuals say that they are doing 'green' publishing, that is probably the best place to start. When you look at 'green' papers and sustainability, you really have to look at everything— from the forest to the paper recycling, to the release of carbon gases {global warming} to the water use, to the production processes' toxic releases to the way the people are treated that are involved in the manufacturing of every step of it— to be a sustainable and produced product. It is something that has very large impact on global warming, the environment, on fresh water, air and our health. So my definition for 'green' publishing really is from the paper manufacturing to the printing and distribution."

~ Archie J. Beaton,
Executive Director - CEO, Chlorine Free Products Association

"The main thing is to reduce the waste and energy used in the publishing industry. That goes from printing on recycled paper to minimizing returns to doing everything we can in a very sustainable way. Reducing the impact of what we do on the earth is important since publishing and printing are a highly intensive process that requires large amounts of energy. It is also inherently a very dirty process in terms of waste and pollution. In our efforts to bring about sustainability, we feel it is incumbent upon all of us to clean up our processes as much as possible."

~ Margo Baldwin,
President and Publisher, Chelsea Green Publishing Company

"I'd say in a nutshell 'green' publishing is about publishers, printers, mills, and others who are involved in the book production industry that are using the most environmentally responsible papers possible. These companies have environmental policies in place to continually reduce their impacts. Then there is the element to 'green' publishing that goes beyond paper that has to do with some new initiatives such as looking at the energy and climate impacts associated with production and finding ways to offset those, whether it is through planting trees and sequestering carbon or carbon offsetting. So 'green' publishing extends beyond just paper."

~ Tyson Miller,
Director, Green Press Initiative

"It is being as environmentally responsible as we possibly can in all areas of our publishing activity, primarily with the materials. I am not only referring to just the text papers, but the paperback covers, the dust jacket papers, the binding, and the cloths that we use. There are specific things about these components as well as the boards which no one ever sees because they are covered with cloth or paper. The binding boards on hardcover books can be addressed separately. One can specify environmentally responsible board be used for their books and even inquire about printing inks, like the soy-based inks we ask a number of our book manufacturers to use. So it is really about being as environmentally responsible as we possibly can be in every area of production and book manufacturing."

~ Tony Crouch,
Director, Design & Production, University of California Press

"I see it as an industry wide effort by publishers, authors, and all the stakeholders which include people like the printers, the book manufacturers, the suppliers, the paper mills, and all of those people in the supply chain. It is an effort by this group to create paper use transformations that will help to conserve natural resources, preserve endangered forests, and protect the indigenous people that could be affected by forestry practices."

~ Myron Marsh
President – CEO, Thomson-Shore, Inc.

"To me, 'green' publishing requires a holistic approach: It is not just one thing. It is not just using recycled paper. It is not just using FSC-certified paper. It is taking an in-depth look at how trees are harvested and understanding how paper relates to the forests and the forest industry around the world. One also needs to understand how the paper is bleached. The inks printers choose to use are important to consider as well: Are they low in volatile organic compounds? Do they contain toxic pigments? How environmentally conscious is the printer overall? And let's think about the publishing cycle itself and how many books are produced. High book returns - as high as 20% or more - plague the book industry. In the magazine sector, the sell-through rate is very low. Over-printing wastes precious resources. So my approach in terms of 'green' publishing is looking at the whole picture and finding alternatives to the traditional processes. Sometimes you have to think outside the box. Sometimes there are no perfect solutions. It is complicated. Publishing 'green' requires a collaborative approach among authors, publishers, printers, and paper mills. We are all in it together. "

~ Deborah Bruner,
Director, Book Publishing Papers, New Leaf Paper

As you can see, each person we asked had a similar yet different perspective of what "green" book publishing means. We find that defining "green" book publishing refers to a holistic or start-to-finish process that holds the opportunity for improvement in each area of the system. You can define what "green" book publishing means to you as you learn about the different facets of how it works.

The Impact of Progress in "Green" Book Publishing

Before we dive into the nuts and bolts of publishing and the choices you have to make your book "green", we thought it might be helpful to provide you with a brief historical look at the publishing industry and how one of the leaders we spoke with has seen his efforts progress over the years.

"When we started our business in December of 1972, initially we started to recycle skids and steel strapping and anything that we could save. I was not so worried about whether we were 'green', but that what we were doing with materials at that point was efficient. We started selling cover board and binding supplies. We added end papers and cover papers in 1976, and started to learn more about how some of the products we were using were being made. Papers in those days were acidic and primarily made using dyes and pigments that were the lowest cost or the most efficient to manufacture within the plant. Not necessarily environmentally friendly.

"After we bought our coating plant in 1979, we learned about chemicals and what went into those products. What was good and what was bad. It is not an instant learning process— you have to work at it. By 1983 to 1984 it all started to come together for us. We knew about acid-free papers, and solvent coatings used for cover materials. By 1986, our company in Pawtucket, RI, was emitting about a hundred tons of emissions into the atmosphere every year. In 1987, I decided, that this was not the way of the future and that we needed to change.

When we coat paper for covers, we take a base paper and put a dark red color on it. Then a clear top coat to protect that coloring. Our base coats have been water based for 70 or 80 years but the top coats were solvent based. The EPA was becoming more involved, and we decided, 'That solvent is not good. Let's try getting rid of it.'

"We talked to some of the suppliers that we used. They all said, 'You can't do that with water based material it's impossible.' We are now in 2007. It has been a long time since 1988 or 1989. We are probably on the seventh generation of improvement, and today we make products that are as good as anything in the world. We started out with a hundred tons of emissions. I think we reduced 27% of these the first year, 54% the second year, and by 2001 we were down to a half a ton.

"In 2002 we were clean. We had some customers that did not like it. It certainly is more difficult to coat and decorate with water than it was with solvent. We just plugged ahead with it. 'It was the way we were going and that was it.' We lost some business, especially one major company. We actually have them back now, but it took a while.

"We started to look at other things such as heavy metals in our coatings. I thought, if you're going to supply material that is going on a children's book, my children did and my grandchildren will occasionally chew on the corner of a book. Well, I don't want them chewing on something that is bad. So we eliminated all heavy metals from our processes.

"We have had to develop our own methods of doing things with water base. We looked at what was bad and eliminated everything we could. We found most people, especially young people in our industry, loved the idea. When we got our opportunity to speak with a customer who was just learning or coming in as a trainee to our business, they thought the information was great.

"Times have changed, and it is important to go forward. I guess for our part of it, we have been doing it for so long that we just take it for granted that this is how everybody should do it."

~ Stephen F. Quill,
Chairman – Ecological Fibers, Inc.

One man's journey through the "green" publishing world sheds light on how thoughtful choices can make a big difference. We all have the opportunity to learn more about what we can change in our businesses that will impact the lives of those close to us and those we do not even know. For example, children everywhere can chew on a book from Ecological Fibers and not be impacted by the heavy metals that are now absent from the books. All this because one man made an educated decision that being "green" was important enough to him.

Go Green!...

In today's book publishing world, there are lots of resources and companies who are prepared to assist you in making your book as "green" as you choose.

Many of the leaders in the "green" book publishing industry have seen these choices emerge because of their efforts to improve their processes for you as an author. They followed their hearts and worked with the advancements that developed in the industry to increase the number of options available to publishers and printers alike.

Each of these leaders would agree that without you, the author, they would never have the opportunity to bring their talents, wisdom, knowledge and experience to the industry. You see, without the author, there is no industry.

All of these companies are prepared to welcome you with open arms into a friendly world of environmentally conscious options to make your book "green".

ESP Tip™ ~ *Stand fast to what you feel is best for you, and have the courage to make choices that resonate with your own "green" interests. Whether big or small, your educated decisions will transform every effort you make as an author and impact millions who read your book.*

PAT Tip™ ~ *Please share this information with other authors you know who might be curious about what "green" book publishing means to them.*

CHAPTER : 2

The Art and Science of "Green" Book Publishing

An art is defined as the creation of beautiful or significant things. A science is a system of knowledge. Scientific research solves problems, answers questions, and provides solutions. "Green" book publishing results in the "eco-llaboration" of art and science.

Creating a book and being an author presents the opportunity for your message and idea to be expressed in a beautiful, holistic package—with a hard or soft cover, colorful endpapers, paper that is friendly towards the environment, and vibrant inks that engage the reader and brighten their perspective.

In this section, we asked the Collective Wisdom Team™ of the "green" book publishing industry, "how do we make THAT 'green'?"™ Here they share their knowledge about each stage of the book publishing process and how a moment of thoughtful consideration can make the difference in the environmental impact felt worldwide when you publish your book.

Today's Green Book Publishing Options:
There Are So Many to Choose From!

When we venture into the publishing world as authors, sometimes we anticipate that the "green" part of "green" book publishing is more complicated than it really is. At times it feels like the information we seek is just too difficult to find or that it is going to take too much time to locate, yet we are always confident that it is out there. We feel as though we just have to find it.

"Asking questions of the publisher and/or doing research to find out which publishers are already using environmentally friendly practices is one of the best starting places. It perpetuates the message and helps support the existing green momentum."

~ Tyson Miller,
Director, Green Press Initiative

We discovered that by asking simple questions, we have been able to quickly get the guidance we need to understand the choices available to make our books "green." We found that asking was the key.

The truth is: there are many options available to you and your publisher to produce your book using ecologically sound practices.

From Start to Finish and From Cover to Cover

The process of book publishing presents many opportunities for authors and publishers to discuss the "green" options available.

"We need every segment of the process to become engaged in being as environmentally responsible and green as possible. Authors traditionally leave the material selection, production, and manufacturing up to the publisher. They are focused, as rightly so, on the content. The publisher is focused on the content—publishing the content—but is responsible for the form. If authors can become engaged in contributing towards the form as well as the content, then there is a push back on the publisher to make their books 'green'. We have seen this taking place here at our press where some authors are specifically asking and requesting that we use environmentally responsible paper for the printing of their books. So colleagues of mine who acquire these manuscripts and work with the authors come to me and ask, 'Is that possible?'

"The authors don't need to necessarily be experts. The authors need to speak to the experts. We need to help them understand it is easy to make anything 'green' anywhere in the spectrum, from a little bit 'green' to all-out 'green'."

~ Tony Crouch,
Director, Design & Production, University of California Press

The spectrum of the process is easy for any author to understand and inquire about. "Green" alternatives are available for any piece of the puzzle. All you have to do is determine how "green" you want your book to be. If you are not sure, ask more questions about each step.

Cover Materials and Endpapers

The main focus of our inquiry about cover materials is focused on the great work we found at Ecological Fibers, Inc.

Stephen F. Quill is the founder and Chairman of the Board of the company. It is through the commitment and efforts of his entire team that Ecological Fibers, Inc. has continued to be true to their philosophy. The company has a long history of using environmentally sound production processes and eliminating harmful chemicals in their plants and products.

Here is an example from Steve about the impact of the choices made for cover materials and endpapers:

"Many people weren't interested in the beginning. I think we have convinced a lot of them — in some cases one at a time — that it is okay to be ecologically sound. Sometimes you explain to people, and they don't understand why it is so important. All of a sudden they get it and their response is great. It's good to do it this way."

> ~ *Stephen F. Quill,*
> *Chairman – Ecological Fibers, Inc.*

Here is a brief list of some of the materials used for covers and the ends of your book. We thought that these short descriptions would be helpful for those of you who really like to know all of the details or just want to prepare yourself for a discussion with your publisher, book manufacturer, printer or book consultant. These short explanations provide you with a quick framework of terms for your conversation to determine how "green" you want the outside of your book to be.

Hardcover book covers include binder board which is mostly graphic board. To avoid confusion, graphic board is just a form of cardboard used with books. Pick up any hardcover book you have in your home, office, school or library and look at it. It is sturdy because it has binder board underneath the front cover, the spine or side of the book, and the back cover. A piece of cloth or paper that includes your cover design is wrapped around these boards and glued together. Some hardcover books have a second piece of paper wrapped around it where the flaps fold inside the book. This is called a dust jacket cover. This thicker piece of paper has been painted and treated with your cover design and then wrapped around the hardcover of the book. But it is not glued to the binder board. So it is the piece of paper that wraps around the book that can fall off easily. Often times, many people use the front or back flap of the dust jacket cover as a "bookmark" to keep their place when they close a book they have not finished reading.

You may be wondering where the "green" part is in all of this. We were told a wonderful story from one of our trusted book manufacturing mentors about why they chose to offer ecologically sound binder board to all of their clients about a decade ago.

"About ten years ago, Tony Crouch at University of California Press came to Thomson-Shore with a strong request that the binder boards used for his project be environmentally friendly, or what is referred to as 100% post-consumer recycled waste. Thomson-Shore did not provide this type of material for its clients on a regular basis. So they charged a small fee to meet the additional costs of three to five cents per book to Tony in order to service this request, and then asked their supplier to furnish this particular binder board to meet Tony's demand.

"Thomson-Shore eventually made a decision to have their supplier provide only this type of binder board for use in all of their manufacturing products. As a result, the additional fee charged to Tony Crouch was dropped since Thomson-Shore elected to use the same binder board supply for every client. If Tony hadn't made this request, we wouldn't have considered using the post-consumer recycled waste binder boards. Today, Thomson-Shore continues to use only 100% post-consumer recycled waste binder board for all of their hardcover book projects.

"A few years ago, the suppliers also made a decision to supply this binder board with these environmental specifications to all its customers—making this a standard industry-wide for most hard back books."

~ David J. Raymond,
Sales Manager-West Region, Thomson-Shore, Inc.

What resulted from one person from one publisher asking for one specific environmental material inspired an entire manufacturing process to change and industry-wide progress. From the supplier to the manufacturer, the insistence of Tony Crouch from University of California Press became a catalyst for decisions that transformed an industry. What Thomson-Shore did during this situation was truly revolutionary. They opted to provide an environmentally sound product to all of their customers, whether it was specifically requested or not.

Tony was willing to pay the small fee of three to five cents per book in order to ensure the environmental integrity of his book products. This story illustrates beautifully the power of a question and a few pennies to make a worldwide difference.

Paperback covers are thicker pieces of paper that are wrapped around your book and glued to the spine. Some are laminated to make the cover stronger and last longer. Laminating allows you to use just about any material for covers and still end up with a nice, glossy finish. However, lamination is not an environmentally sound process as it emits Volatile Organic Compounds, or VOCs, that are harmful to human beings and the earth. Volatile Organic Compounds contribute to air and water pollution when they escape into the air through evaporation. Some laminating uses large amounts of adhesives which create an issue during the recycling process. You can use a coated paper for your cover to potentially avoid this step and make your book more environmentally sound. You can ask your publisher, book manufacturer, or printer if the paperback cover for your book uses lamination and whether they are using eco-friendly paper and ink.

Endpapers are used to complete the inside of the front and back cover of your hardcover book. These papers are glued to the binder boards immediately inside the front and back of the book. So these actually become the first and last page of your hardcover book because one half of the endpaper is glued to the binder board and the other half becomes the first page of the book. This is the final step to secure your cover to the book because the endpaper is glued to the cover and the binder board. Companies like Rainbow® from Ecological Fibers, Inc. offer a spectrum of colors and textures to choose from to match the look and feel that you want in your book. Paperback books do not use endpapers, so you will not need to include these in your discussion if your book is a paperback.

Rainbow® is a large supplier of endpapers to many of the manufacturers in the book publishing and printing industry. As a result, these components of your book may inadvertently be ecologically sound due to the supply used from Rainbow® in the manufacturing of your book. Rainbow® produces papers using 100% solvent free processes. This may come to you as a pleasant surprise that there is a good possibility that your book would already be pre-disposed to "green" processes. This is often a well-kept secret in the book publishing world. So just ask your publisher, printer, book manufacturer or consultant if the endpapers you are using are eco-friendly.

Side materials include binder board for the spine if it is a hardcover book as well as the glue that is used to bind the book together. Pick up your hardcover book again and this time – look at the side of the book. Just like the spine that runs down the center of your back as a human being where the major connections to the rest of your body meet, the spine of a book is where all of the pages and the cover are attached. This connecting of the papers and the cover is what is meant by the "binding of the book." There is no other place on the book or inside the book where this binding can take place. A long time ago, the pages were "stitched" into the spine using thread. These days, glue is the most common form used for binding. Textbooks for schools are the only books that still tend to use the thread stitching method.

The glue used for binding is not currently environmentally friendly and is one of the biggest areas for improvement. Many in the "green" book publishing world are aware of this and share the perspective that a solution needs to be further explored in order to make progress in this area.

Recommendation: You may want to bring this guide with you to the discussion with your publisher, book manufacturer, printer or book consultant so you can refer to this information when discussing your cover materials and endpapers.

Paper

Every book except an electronic book requires paper in order for someone else to read your thoughts, ideas and clever sentences. Paper is a major component of every book and tends to be the focus of most "green" discussions in the book publishing industry. In fact, when you approach your "green" questions with your publisher, book manufacturer, printer or book consultant, the first topic they will probably talk about is the paper.

There are lots of terms that describe the different types of paper available to use during the process of printing your book. Post-consumer recycled, percent recycled, acid-free, chlorine free, and FSC certified are some of the words that will be mentioned when someone tells you about their "green" papers. Please refer to the glossary for thoughtful explanations of the different types of these papers. Here our industry experts comment about some of these and why it is important to ask specifically about the paper for your book.

Recycled paper

"What we consider to be recycled paper is paper that is generally and honestly taken from the waste stream—meaning somebody, a consumer, used it for its initial intended purpose. They then put it in a recycling bin where it got collected with other paper to be bundled and baled so it could be sent to a paper mill where it got made into paper once again. Old fibers that were used in the process of making paper went through their intended purpose and then got made into paper again. That, in the true sense, is recycling.

"There has always been a misunderstanding because there are many providers of recycled products in the paper industry. There is a lot of loosely thrown about terminology that says paper is recycled or it contains recycled material. It could be as simple as in the manufacturing of paper in a paper mill. In the beginning of the paper making process, a large roll of paper gets produced. Paper gets produced from fibers being blended with water. In the process of making paper, a lot of times that big, big roll of paper which could be forty feet wide and thousands of feet long ends up breaking while being produced. When it breaks in the manufacturing process, the paper is again deposited into the pulping vat under the mill floor where it is re-pulped to become paper again. It is really not recycled. It is using the resource being used initially to create the paper. It is not recovered from the waste stream. It is really not recycled even though it gets labeled 'recycled'.

"This mis-labeling is misleading and the recycled paper is of no environmental value."

~ Tom Kemper,
CEO & Founder, Dolphin Blue

Why is recycled paper so important?

Here is what one industry expert shared with us about what she learned when she found out about the whole printing and paper process:

"A lot of people don't think about how books are made. I certainly didn't when I started my first publishing job. Educating myself about the printing and paper industries has at times been laborious as well as frightening – but always educational. Both industries have historically created a fair amount of pollution and contributed to environmental degradation. For example, for a long time paper mills were the number one source of dioxin pollution in waterways in the U.S. (Note: Dioxin is considered the most dangerous carcinogen to mankind.) So I started thinking about how I could buy paper that was more environmentally friendly. The next step was educating others about eco-friendly options – if I could do it, I figured so could everyone else."

~ Deborah Bruner,
Director, Book Publishing Papers, New Leaf Paper

Does recycled paper cost more?

"If you and I were to sit down and seriously analyze that issue, I think we may come to the conclusion that recycled paper does not cost more.

"If we look at the environmental costs, costs to human health, costs to habitat of fellow species, and societal costs, I think we could honestly say recycled paper does not cost more.

"That being said, yes, the receipt from purchases made at the register reflect recycled paper costing more, but we know that is not the final price we pay. Unfortunately, we human beings don't look at the whole picture when we make our purchase decisions, and don't seem interested in doing so."

~ Tom Kemper,
CEO & Founder, Dolphin Blue

As described above by our experts, papers which are "post-consumer recycled" (PCR), like those we have been referring to here, come from the post-consumer waste (PCW) stream such as the office paper you recycle. Therefore, the PCW or PCR letters are clues to help you recognize that these papers use fewer trees than non-recycled papers. When you see "100% PCW" or "100% PCR" describing the paper you are proposing to use for your book, you will know that no new trees were cut down to make the paper. No virgin fibers were used to produce the paper.

As an author, when you specify post-consumer paper, besides reducing the amount of trees logged for paper production, you help grow the market for recycled products and actually ensure the viability of recycling programs. Did you know that your choice in paper had such a rippling effect?

Before we take you from the paper to the ink, there is a bit of confusion we would like to clear up about the term "acid-free." In fact, we needed to ask a few of our Collective Wisdom Team™ members to assist us with this because we got confused when we asked for help.

Archie J. Beaton from the Chlorine Free Products Association helped us resolve the mystery about acid-free papers. As we found out, "acid-free" refers to the chemistry of the paper and how it is treated. It uses alkaline chemicals to support the longevity of the paper, causing it to withstand hundreds of years of wear and tear without yellowing or fading. So "acid-free" has virtually nothing to do with anything "green". This term is neither eco-friendly or eco-harmful. It just means that your pages are going to last longer, which is good for your message.

Ink

While most people know that it takes ink to make a book, many may not be aware that there are different kinds of ink that take your thoughts and put them on paper.

"All printing inks contain solvents such as alcohol and other hydrocarbons in varying levels. Before the 1960's inks made from vegetable oils were commonplace in all areas of printing. However, with the boom in petroleum availability, mineral-based inks became cheaper and out-performed vegetable-based inks both in the printing room and the market.

"Today, soy inks are thought by many printers to be more forgiving, making it easier to get a high quality job from older equipment. Soy inks have broad applicability; although commonly used in lithograph printing processes for newspapers, books, and magazines, they are also effective to use for commercial printing applications.

"Water-based inks are rare, and often use dyes (with an organic rather than mineral basis).

"The above information from DolphinBlue.com was gleaned from an excellent article entitled 'Think Ink' that is published by Sustainable Business Network (SBN) of New Zealand. Our thanks go to Joss Debreceny, Communications Manager for SBN, for granting us permission to republish SBN's article."

~ Tom Kemper,
CEO & Founder, Dolphin Blue

"Inks have different components, including pigments, as well as petroleum or vegetable oil. When you replace petroleum with a vegetable oil, whether it's soybean oil or tung oil or another kind of plant-based oil, what you do in the printing process is reduce the amount or percentage of volatile organic compounds (VOCs) that are released from the printing plant into the air. VOCs contribute to smog. Petroleum-based inks have much higher VOCs than vegetable-based inks. The EPA monitors what printing plants (and other industries) emit into the air, so by using low VOC inks a company reduces its air pollution.

"In terms of printing, web-based printers tend to have more trouble with soy-based inks because they don't dry as quickly. Petroleum-based inks dry very quickly because they contain certain solvents. Printing is an industry that really runs 24/7 and the ability to produce high quality printed materials in fast time frames is paramount to a printer's success. Soy-based inks are much more successful on sheet-fed presses, because such presses run slower and the longer drying times don't pose the same problem they do for web presses.

"Soy-based inks really work very well in color printing because an ink base of a clear vegetable oil rather than petroleum (which is by nature black) allows colors to pop. Conversely, a true black can sometimes be hard to "hit" with a vegetable-based ink precisely because of the absence of petroleum, but I think most printers have found ways to work around this.

"In thinking about inks, the other thing to be aware of above and beyond whether inks are vegetable-based is the fact that up until recently many pigments contained heavy metals such as cadmium and barium, to name just a couple. It took the industry a long time to find environmentally friendly replacements for those heavy metals. Some of these heavy metals were on the EPA's seven deadliest heavy metals list.

"If you have ever been in a printing plant, you know ink is everywhere. You have waste ink and you have to think about how printers dispose of it. Much or all of it has to be carted away to a hazardous waste landfill. You can't just dump it down a drain. Print operators get ink on their hands, and if the inks are toxic in some way, they are ingesting that toxicity. As I've said before, 'green' publishing involves looking at everybody and everything that touches your product."

~ Deborah Bruner,
Director, Book Publishing Papers, New Leaf Paper

Environmental Statements

Environmental statements are issued by companies and individuals. These are drafted based on the proclamation of the organization or person of their environmentally sound practices. For example, Ecological Fibers, Inc., released their formal environmental statement this year. So even though they have been using ecologically sound practices for years, this statement was released formally as part of their global communication.

Eco-Audits

According to Wikipedia, an audit is an evaluation of an organization, system, process, project or product. It is performed by a competent, independent and objective person or persons, known as auditors or accountants.

When an eco-audit is performed, it becomes an evaluation of the environmental practices of an organization, system, process, project or product. When an eco-audit is conducted for books, like the ones in the front of this book from the Green Press Initiative and New Leaf Paper, the results of your choices and how they impact the environment are calculated. Specifically, the effects of savings in trees, water, energy, solid waste and greenhouse gases are shown in numerical statistics to help the author understand the significance of their decision. Here is a brief explanation about an example of an eco-audit and how it is calculated:

"The Eco Audit helps you tell your leadership story—in a way that's transparent and supported by fact.

"The environmental benefits stated in the Eco Audit are calculated based on research by Environmental Defense and members of the Paper Task Force, who studied the environmental impacts of the paper industry. They performed life-cycle analyses of post-consumer waste vs. virgin fiber, which revealed the tangible environmental benefits of using post-consumer recycled content instead of virgin content. The Paper Task Force members included senior executives from Environmental Defense, Duke University, Johnson & Johnson, McDonald's, Prudential Insurance and Time Inc. For more information about Environmental Defense and the Paper Task Force report, go to www.environmentaldefense.org and site search on 'Paper Task Force.'"

~ Deborah Bruner,
Director, Book Publishing Papers, New Leaf Paper

When we received our Eco-Audits for this book, we received one for our cover and a separate one for the interior text pages. We wanted to know what the total environmental impact of our book production choices were, so we added these two audits together on our own to get the complete figures.

You can receive an Eco-Audit for any portion of your book that you choose to make "green" so you can gain a better understanding of the value and results of your production decisions on the environment. Determine how "green" you want to be, then use an Eco-Audit to calculate your win-win for you and the planet.

Certification Information

There are several certifications that are available for paper used in the book publishing industry.

Here is a global view of them from Tyson Miller along with a brief background about the Forest Stewardship Council which is referred to as FSC.

"A Brief Background on the FSC:

The Forest Stewardship Council (FSC) is an international non-profit forest certification organization with members from over 70 countries whose interests reflect a unique combination of biodiversity conservation, environmental protection, civil society, indigenous rights, and wood and paper production. The FSC program is widely accepted as setting the highest standards for protecting people and the environment while allowing for the deliberate and careful logging of forests to support the continued use of the planet's most renewable resource —

forests. Since 1993 FSC has certified forest operations in over 70 countries and has been a key driver in the transformation of the forest industry's logging practices.

"A Global View of Certifications and Why the FSC is so Important:

"FSC stands for the Forest Stewardship Council. There is a variety of different forest management certification systems out there. You have the Sustainable Forestry Initiative, or SFI. There is the Canadian Standards Association, or CSA. The Programme for the Endorsement of Forest Certification schemes, the PEFC, is a global organization including members from Europe, Australia, Canada, and the U.S. Then there is the FSC which is at the top of all of these certifications.

"The reason why the FSC is at the top is because the FSC ensures that any land use disputes with indigenous people or social concerns must be resolved with an extensive space solution for all sides engaged in order for that forest management area to get the FSC classification. This is really important because it mitigates social concerns. Another reason is that it ensures that endangered forests are being adequately identified and set aside to protect them. In addition, under the FSC system there are no more forest conversions taking beautiful and bio-diverse forests and converting them to chemically managed single species pine plantations. This is really key.

"There is a variety of other principles as to why FSC is better. It is a global system and all the others are more regional. FSC is developed and defined by the conservation community whereas others are developed by industry."

~ *Tyson Miller,*
Director, Green Press Initiative

FSC paper comes from new trees or what is referred to as virgin fiber. It is the preferred alternative when 100% post-consumer recycled paper is not available.

Processed Chlorine Free Certification

There is another term that is referred to when it comes to defining paper and certifications called "processed chlorine free."

Chlorine is a chemical used in the bleaching, or whitening, of papers. Chlorine is a dangerous chemical that gets into our waterways. According to the Chlorine Free Products Association web site, "Chlorine bleaches out Life".

Archie J. Beaton of the Chlorine Free Products Association offered us the following perspective of these chlorine processes:

"To make one single 8½ by 11 inch sheet of paper using chlorine chemistry requires more than 13 ounces of water for every single 8½ by 11 inch sheet. So that means more than a good sized can of Coke is needed for every sheet that you use for copying. If it was produced with chlorine free technology, it would require less than two ounces of water. So there is a tremendous difference in just the raw water usage."

~ Archie J. Beaton,
Executive Director - CEO, Chlorine Free Products Association

So, chlorine free papers protect us from chlorine and from wasting water.

The certification process of chlorine-free papers requires that companies use ways to whiten paper without using chlorine.

"We actually introduced the first processed chlorine free certification through the Chlorine Free Products Association in 1996, and it has been evolving ever since. We do a review to make sure that companies have no current or pending environmental permit violations. We also are researching to see if they are a financially sound company. When we do these audits, we help the manufacturers take a look at their own process to see where they can actually save money and reduce their environmental footprint.

"The audits we provide for pulp and paper companies are the most stringent in the world. This offers publishers an opportunity to use products that have the least environmental impact on the papers they use without having to do that research themselves."

~ Archie J. Beaton,
Executive Director - CEO, Chlorine Free Products Association

For more information about these certifications and others, please refer to the Certifications section of this book. You can get the information you are seeking directly from each organization's website.

The Green Spectrum

As you can see from this chapter, there are many options offered by the book publishing industry to make all the parts of your book "green".

We know this chapter is also a bit scientific – or what we affectionately refer to as the "Green Guide Gook™." We feel it is important because it provides you with insights about how "green" you can be.

What we want you to know is that the book publishing industry is prepared to support you at every stage of production so your book can use environmentally sound processes every step of the way.

ESP Tip™ ~ *Just like the smorgasbord of life, you can choose from a multitude of options in the "green" publishing world. Make educated decisions about how "green" you want your book to be. If you are unsure about what is available, refer to this helpful guide to the spectrum of possibilities. Share your "green" choices with others who might be interested in learning how to make their books "green" using this same scale. It is easy to make your book "green" when you follow your heart and choose the right components for you.*

PAT Tip™ ~ *As you trek through the "green" book publishing process, remember to take time to consider the information you have read. Please flip through and reread sections of this chapter. Write down what parts of the spectrum you want to be "green" in your book and ear-mark the corner of the pages for easy reference when you speak with your publishing team. You can write your thoughts and notes in the My "Green" Book Publishing Notes section in the back of this book. Get ready and enjoy the "green" impact your book is about to make in the world.*

CHAPTER : 3

The Ones to Watch in the "Green" Book Publishing World

A̲ll of the members of our Collective Wisdom Team™, as we affectionately refer to them, have grown up in the "green" book publishing world. Each of them has a unique story about what inspired them to get involved so many years ago.

During this chapter, we want to introduce you to each of the individuals on our Collective Wisdom Team™ so you can learn about their background, how they got started with "green" publishing, some brief information about what they do and why we find their guidance so valuable.

Tyson Miller, Director, Green Press Initiative

"My major in college was environmental studies. While I was finishing up school, I first got into environmental work by doing a documentary called 'Generation Earth' that profiled successful environmental education programs around the

U.S. The purpose of the documentary was so that they could be models for other schools. I got four stars from the NSTA (National Science Teachers Association).

"I had to go make money so I didn't really promote it very much. That got me into the world of environmental education work and developing programs in Los Angeles.

"You see, I was pretty frustrated, upset and concerned with the fact endangered forests were being cut down to make paper when we have other solutions like recycled paper available. Paper makes up close to 30% of what is in our landfills. It is just nonsensical, especially given what trees and forests do for indigenous and rural communities as well as for balancing climate, providing habitats, and all sorts of wonderful things. So I got started with developing the Recycled Products Cooperative and later developed the Green Press Initiative (GPI).

"I founded it and I run it. I wear lots of different hats, but there are two other folks that work with me part-time — Erin Johnson and Todd Pollak. All three of us help publishers, printers and mills and others to take steps in the right direction. Through GPI, I also helped to found the Environmental Paper Network with about eight other organizations. It has grown since 2002 into a one hundred organization-wide network with different sorts of agreements for organizations working to support each other and to advance common environmental goals. There is a European Environmental Network now, and there is an Indonesian one starting up too. There is also a South American one in process, so that is really gratifying to see that taking root. We are trying to do things that address macro level issues. We just coordinated a round table in New York with fifty industry corporate stakeholders with the premise being: 'what are we going to do to ensure a viable recycled fiber infrastructure with all the new demands coming up online.' So we work on those sorts of macro level issues as well. That is how the Environmental Paper Network and Green Press Initiative play an active role.

"It gives me a sense of fulfillment that I am doing something small that might be a model for other sectors. I am starting to see that now in the works in the magazine sector. They are looking at some of the things that we are doing in the book sector, and they are trying to replicate them. So I think it just sustains me to know that I'm doing something that is trying to bring about some positivity."

Myron Marsh, President – CEO, Thomson-Shore, Inc.

"Personally I am committed to 'green' publishing because I love the outdoors. I love the planet. I have been somewhat of a follower of the philosophy I learned back in the '70s when I heard R. Buckminster Fuller speak about 'spaceship earth' – that we are kind of a contained capsule and we are doing all this to ourselves. It hit home so I started changing my own personal practices around the same time and taking an interest. But at the same time, I'm a capitalist so I'm a business person. Profitability is a way of keeping score to measure whether you are moving forward or not. I think there is an advantage to using that to also bring about change. So personally I like seeing the two pieces work together. If Thomson-Shore can use its purchasing power to leverage things and move them in the right direction, then I think that's a good thing.

"Prior to becoming the CEO of Thomson-Shore, I was working in a position in manufacturing for another company in a different industry. I had an interest in leading an organization like this because it was employee-owned and I liked the culture of the organization. I felt that I could actually switch industries. I'm very passionate about books, as is my wife. Throughout all the years we've been married, I could never bring home a product to her because, really, what would she do with an injection molding machine part or something? So she was ecstatic about the opportunity every now and then that I might bring a book home or that she could attend a book industry event. These were all reasons why I went into this industry.

"At Thomson-Shore, we would see ourselves as teachers. That may sound odd, but we spend a lot of time with all the constituents and people in the supply chain. Whether it be authors or publishers or paper mills, we help them to understand how we can move forward and protect our natural resources. We show them how to be smarter about how we consume paper and other items that affect the environment. So we do things like work with paper mills as a go-between, whether it is authors or publishers and the mill to actually create a paper that is acceptable to the marketplace. We want a quality paper that also runs in a production environment so that we don't lose time or economics in manufacturing. Our goal is to be able to put a paper that is available for book printing that is of equal quality to anything else at a price parity so there is not a penalty for people that are buying these papers. There is a lot of behind-the-scenes work for us to do that takes a lot of time and a lot of testing. But it is a commitment, and it is a worthwhile commitment. The other thing we do is we challenge our competition. So sometimes it can be subtle in the way we are offering something that they don't have and they have to play catch-up. I don't know if that is subtle but that is not a direct route. Sometimes it is in meetings where we challenge them. That is a little more of a direct route. We say, 'You are kind of beating around the bush with this policy, and you are counting your pre-consumer waste. You should be counting your post-consumer waste, so what gives?' So we challenge our competition and other members of the industry. We encourage the marketplace. We work with both authors and publishers, encouraging them to use recycled sheets. At the same time since we have converted all of our house products that we inventory here to recycled papers, even somebody that is not that interested in the green movement is going to get a recycled sheet when they order a house sheet. So we either get them directly or indirectly. Those are some of the things that we do to support the effort and move in the right direction.

"As educators for publishers or an author, we help you through the process of paper selection, what works well, pricing and those kinds of things. But there is a whole other world that I think we spend even more time in educating — and that is back to the supply chain where we're educating paper mills. We are using our dollars and our purchasing power to do that. We are educating the suppliers. Every year we host a supplier day where we have all our key suppliers come in to Michigan so we can talk about our goals. Our discussions are about the environment, not just paper materials. We challenge our suppliers. We are always educating them as to the reasons why this is good for their business too.

"This is a very open company. It is sort of unique in the fact that it is 100 percent employee-owned. Our employees have a lot of tenure here and are very involved. They challenge me and the leadership group here. We are all in this together. It is a very supportive environment.

"The business was founded that way by Ned Thomson and Harry Shore. They had a belief that people should have a good place to work. With that founding principle, the business is celebrating our 35th anniversary. We have been able to sustain that. It is a part of the culture that we have to keep going.

"I think you have to walk the talk. You can't be doing the effort in the publishing world and limit it to primarily this paper recycling effort that we have been focused on. That's really an offshoot of all these other pieces. We have been recycling everywhere in our company. We have been trying to reduce spoilage during production and trying to get publishers not to overbuy printing. This way we don't end up having to pulp what they don't sell. We have been working that angle for years."

Stephen F. Quill, Chairman – Ecological Fibers, Inc.

"We have been the driving force for 'green' cover materials used in publishing for the last twenty years. If you believe it is right then you have an obligation to move that way. It was easy in this particular area of our business to have moved into the 'green' publishing arena over the years. Not only do we think it is good for our employees and customers, ultimately it would be good financially and our world in general. It is really our employees who made that happen, and they have many reasons to be very proud of their efforts.

"For me personally, I have been fortunate enough to fish in Alaska, Northern Quebec, Labrador, Russia, and all over the rest of the U.S. I have been in the woods, hunting in places that most people will never see. I have spent a fair amount of my time outdoors. I like the outdoors, and I believe that we should manage our environment. I like seeing rivers, falls and wild water along with forests that haven't ever been touched.

"I guess what we do is, try to make sure that some of this stays for future generations. I look at it like this: think about when you are releasing emissions out into our atmosphere — that is not right. With solvent, the best you could do was clean about 85 percent of your emissions. Why isn't it better to not have any emission at all — it is. If you can just answer simple questions, maybe the hardest problems get a little easier. What we have learned is that when you get a group of people together, that want to solve a problem, they can do it. In our company 'I saw that it can happen.'"

Deborah Bruner, Director, Book Publishing Papers, New Leaf Paper

"When I graduated from college in the early 1980's I just kind of landed in publishing and discovered I really loved it. Back then, to me being involved in environmental issues meant reading *Sierra Club Magazine* and following Green Peace activities. I was one of those little postcard activists (signing petitions and sending them off in the mail to senators and presidents). Now there are email campaigns, but back then it was postcard campaigns. I think at one point I belonged to ten or twelve different environmental organizations and gave the post office a lot of business.

"In the early 1990's I was production manager at Jossey-Bass Publishers and my boss one day asked me to investigate soy-based inks. We were already using recycled paper (back then that was paper with 10% PCW, a big deal) and my boss wanted to do something further. I had no clue what soy-based ink was. I had no idea it would open up all kinds of doors. I had no idea it would sort of ignite this passion for learning about something that is relatively scientific in a lot of ways. I have never considered myself to be somebody really interested in scientific issues but in learning about soy-based inks and bleaching practices or even forestry issues, I became very attached to finding eco-friendly solutions and how those could be practiced at the corporate level (rather than at the 'postcard activist' level). The more you learn, the more you realize you need to learn. It's endless, but always fascinating.

"I love to try to educate other publishers (or authors) on eco-friendly publishing. What can be frustrating is trying to correct the many misconceptions that exist when it comes to logging or bleaching issues or whatever the issue may be. Eco-friendly publishing is complicated and there are lots of 'paper myths.' Still, I believe in what I do and I'm happy the publishing industry is being receptive to 'green' publishing. Book publishing can have a profound influence on the environment.

"Jeff Mendelsohn founded New Leaf Paper in 1998. As a true visionary he wanted to do something that would not only help the environment but also be a sustainable business model. New Leaf Paper is very unique as a paper company in that we specialize only in recycled papers—papers with the best overall environmental benefits. The mills we partner with create beautiful recycled papers. New Leaf Paper is 100% committed to our mission of inspiring a shift toward sustainability in the paper industry, and this commitment shines through in every one of our product lines.

"I joined New Leaf Paper after being a customer of the company. Part of my role at New Leaf Paper is to really try and educate and consult with authors and production managers to help them decide on the best paper for their projects. I help them understand the environmental ramifications of their purchasing decisions and I help them lessen their company's ecological footprint. It is encouraging to see so many people get inspired by this process."

Tony Crouch, Director, Design & Production,
University of California Press

"'Green' publishing was initially brought to my attention by my good friend and colleague, Deborah Bruner, who at that time was the production manager at Cornell University Press. She knew a man by the name of George Pappas, who is no longer in the paper industry. It was the combination of a presentation that George made with the support of Deborah that really brought 'green' publishing to my attention—and it was like a wake-up call. I thought, 'Wow, this is really something that we should make a commitment to at our press.' It made perfect sense to me to do this. From there on, I just became more enthusiastic about it, more passionate about making these commitments, and kept telling other colleagues at other university presses and some trade houses. I was involved for several years with going to Publishers Association of the West meetings, formerly known as the Rocky Mountain Publishers Association, and giving talks to them about different things. I would judge their book show and talk with them about offset book manufacturing and what you can and can't do. I gradually started including comments about the paper and the materials used, and I think a lot of people in book production didn't realize the power of 'green' publishing. I hesitate to use the word 'power', but maybe there's an element of that in there.

"University of California Press is a member of the AAUP, which stands for the Association of American University Presses. The AAUP has about just over 100 members, primarily in the U.S., with some memberships across Canada and a few affiliates overseas. Every year, the production managers of the university presses have an annual meeting. I would say about eight years ago I became personally acquainted with the need to take into consideration post-consumer waste, recycled content, and responsible chlorine-free pulping of the wood, and the need to avoid the devastation to the environment and wildlife habitat as a result of clear cutting. All those things were brought to my attention by several people, and I just latched onto it right away. I could see this was the way to go. We became one of the frontrunners, along with Deborah Bruner, who was the production manager at Cornell University Press at that time. She was the East Coast proponent, and I was the West Coast. We were working with a couple of paper mills at that time, and we really pushed to have this category of text papers made for many of our books. At that time, there was some resistance from the paper companies, who had various opinions about us. In their world, they don't make a little bit of paper this way and then a little bit of paper that way. They want to make tons and tons of paper to a given weight, shade, opacity, and then make tons and tons of another variant paper. So their initial response to us was often, 'Well, there's no demand for it, so why should we make it? If there's no demand, we can't just make tons of this paper and stick it away in a warehouse somewhere on the off chance that we might sell it. Tell us there's a demand for it, and we'll make it— we'll supply it.' Well, that took several years of talking with colleagues at other university presses, explaining the merits of using these kinds of papers, even the dangers of not doing so. They have been wonderfully supportive over the years, as have many of our valued book manufacturers and component printers. Deborah Bruner founded the AAUP Eco-Task Force to address these initial concerns throughout our association. It is currently hosted and has been expanded by Julia Fauci, Design and Production Manager at Northern Illinois University Press. The whole subject, however, was in its infancy during this time period. Many of us didn't really know that this was an issue that was waiting to be addressed. Beyond our own association the commercial trade group, The Association of American Publishers, the AAP based in New York, formed a working group that is addressing the use of environmentally responsible and post-consumer waste content book text papers. This may also be a partial result of an increasing percentage of authors becoming aware of the options opening up and putting pressure on the publishers by asking, 'If you're going to publish my next book, you are going to have to print it on an environmentally responsible paper, whether it is totally chlorine-free, virgin paper, or whether it is post-consumer-waste PCF, recycled stock.

"From my standpoint, it's very important to me that we all understand as authors and as publishers that we are all really working together. This is where I really see a lot of value in a green conversation happening between the author and the publisher.

"In my capacity here as director for the design, production, and manufacturing of all our books, I do have a significant role to play in the selection of all the materials that are used in our books. When we launch a book into the production stream, we make a determination on a title-by-title basis as to the paper that will be used for the printing of that book and how the binding will take place. We do give our book manufacturers individual print work and binding orders, and they detail exactly the paper, the binding cloth, the board, everything. The book manufacturers that we work with have multi-year contracts with us that are put into place with our Purchasing Department colleagues several years back. These contracts and commitments, in turn, allow those book manufacturers to go to the paper industry and order truckload quantities of the papers that we require at prices per ton that are advantageous to them and to us. They store those papers knowing that we have a steady flow of orders coming in for their use. Then they replenish them on a cyclical basis. I also work with the paper mills very actively because I like to know what they are up to. We keep our fingers on the pulse to the extent that we possibly can. I have worked with colleagues here to acquaint them with the advantages of being involved in 'green' publishing. I think a lot of them now get it and are very supportive of it. By the same token, as I said, I've given a lot of presentations and talks to various groups over the last eight years. You know, converts can be the worst kind, 'Thou shalt use this paper or else you are damned, it's a balancing act'."

Margo Baldwin, President and Publisher,
Chelsea Green Publishing Company

"I co-founded the company with my husband and have been doing this ever since we have been in publishing. When we first started, it was an attempt to try to produce books that would make things better and help change the world. It has just gotten more focused on sustainable living over the history of the company. It was our desire to have an impact to change things for the better. At the same time, we wanted to produce beautiful books and inspire people.

"I have written a few articles about 'green' publishing for *Publishers' Weekly*, the trade magazine. We are being as public as we can and challenging other publishers and book sellers to come along with us."

Archie J. Beaton, Executive Director - CEO, Chlorine Free Products Association

"My background is that I have a Bachelors of Science in Print Marketing. It is kind of amazing since as I was going to college there was never any mention about chlorine chemistry and bleaching. I took bleaching chemistry, and I also took paper and production. In fact, after college, my first job was working in a print factory. So my background is in printing. I worked in the packaging and printing industry for twenty years before I started the Chlorine Free Products Association.

"I was giving a speech at the US EPA's International Symposium on Pollution Prevention in the Manufacture of Pulp & Paper in 1992 in Washington, DC. At that program, I was given the opportunity to speak before around five thousand people, all in the pulp and paper industry. At that time, I worked for a small mill out of upstate New York that was the first chlorine free mill in North America. When I put my presentation together, we had limits as to the kinds of things that we could talk about. You couldn't talk about human health and how one industry was impacting another. Being the kind of individual that I am, that was what my entire speech was about. So as I got up to give the speech, we had people from *Time Magazine* and all over the world there. As soon as I started giving the speech about what benefits were coming with this, I went into the human health aspect of it and how one industry is affecting the life of others.

"The speech was about a place called the Howe Sound, which is north of Vancouver, BC. In Howe Sound, the Native Americans there were, in fact, not able to live their lifestyle anymore. The pulp mill was polluting the Sound so much that they could no longer harvest the fish or the shellfish or any of the crustaceans that were there. So when I started giving that talk, all of a sudden, out of nowhere, an International Paper representative came down to the front of the podium and began pacing back and forth. He told the EPA administration I wasn't allowed to talk about this. Then all of a sudden shortly after that, a Weyerhaeuser representative, a Georgia Pacific representative, and three others were standing in front of my podium looking at me and inferring that I could not say those kinds of things. As the EPA administrator started to stand, I decided it was time to go back to my speech which I was allowed to talk about. I finished my speech, and I left the auditorium. As I left the auditorium, a gentleman came up to me and said, 'Archie, you did so well in presenting these issues, we think you should represent our side of the story.' And that is how the CFPA (Chlorine Free Products Association) got started. That, and a couple thousand dollars of my own money.

"My 'greening' aspect is any time I have the opportunity to speak before an audience, I need to explain that supporting single attributes certifications like forestry, recycling, etc will not create a Sustainable Future. I believe I can really have a positive impact on book publishing in regard to how they green their paper procurements by providing a Sustainability Index on which to judge paper. Now you can judge a book by the cover — look for the TCF/PCF marks."

Tom Kemper, CEO & Founder, Dolphin Blue

"I began Dolphin Blue in 1994, as a result of a 1992 personal experience with the failure we call recycling — where we put things in bins, close our eyes, and imagine we have done the world some good by recycling. In reality, most of what goes in recycling bins never makes it into becoming a product. It either gets dumped in a landfill or incinerated. There isn't enough product being made with the recovered materials we put in the bins. There just isn't enough of a consumer base buying products made of recycled material, nor, demanding through those purchases, that products be made of recycled materials.

"In 1992 I did the first public recycling event at the Shakespeare Festival in Dallas. It is an outdoor summer festival with Shakespeare performances on stage nightly in a city park in Dallas. I spent three and a half weeks collecting all kinds of materials — No. 1 and No. 2 plastics, brown, clear, and green glass, metals and aluminum cans. As the picnickers spread their blankets on the lawn, watching the night's performance, I saw an opportunity to educate people about how they could recycle. I set up bins indicating with signage what goes in the each bin. I had my share of pulling chicken bones from beer bottles and cigarette butts from coke cans. That education was a real eye opener for me because I didn't want to be sorting through people's trash. I figured recycling could be one of those things where you just put it in bins, bag it up, and take it to a processor. Well, after I got done with three and a half weeks of sorting, collecting and bagging up all of this material, I couldn't find anybody that wanted it. It basically had no value. I kept asking the question, 'Why not?' Finally, I found a scrap dealer in South Dallas that took everything off my hands. As I handed over the goods, I asked him, 'Will you please assure me that you won't landfill this stuff?' He said, 'I will sit on it until the markets come around.' I thought about this, and a bell went off. I said, 'What does that mean 'I will sit on it until the markets come around'?' From an economic standpoint a product has no value unless it was being utilized as a resource. Until the markets were in alignment with what was intended for the use of these materials, or reuse of it, it just wasn't going to make sense for anyone to take it. It didn't have any value. So I started looking at the whole issue of what was available in the marketplace. Were people buying products made from recycled materials? Were people looking for 'recycled'? I started to make some determinations as to the viability of my starting a business and being able to make a go of it. It took us twelve years to make a profit, but finally in that twelfth year we became profitable. Now we are off to the races making money providing office supplies and printed paper products made of post consumer recycled materials – and doing the world some good at the same time."

These stories demonstrate the various ways our Collective Wisdom Team™ members became interested and involved in "green" publishing. We found their stories fascinating and inspirational.

As we continue to meet more individuals in the "green" book publishing industry, we look forward to growing our Collective Wisdom Team™ exponentially over the next few years.

ESP Tip™ ~ Anyone at any time can spark an interest in learning more about how to get involved with "green" publishing practices. There are so many people in the industry who are ready and willing to assist you.

PAT Tip™ ~ Please have a conversation with your publishing team and refer to the Resources in the back of this guidebook. Engage one of them in a friendly conversation to clarify questions you have about how your book can be produced with the support of knowledgeable "green" experts.

CHAPTER : 4

Visions of the Future for Eco-Friendly Book Publishing

"Green" book publishing has a vibrant future. There is so much more that is unfolding in this industry. It is very encouraging to all of us in the book publishing world.

We asked each of the members of our Collective Wisdom Team™ to share their vision of the future of "green" book publishing so we can get a glimpse of what we all have to look forward to.

Tyson Miller, Director, Green Press Initiative

"I see GPI staying involved and continuing to do what we do best to help these shifts take place in whatever way we can. I have other ideas and projects I am developing right now. My commitment is to keep this program going and maintaining its effectiveness. I see our program being a bit more embraced — as more of an industry honed organization with an advisory board from some of the largest and smallest publishers and other stakeholders. I want to go out with a survey that identifies what publishers want as well as what others want and need to determine how we can be of the most value. I want to move a bit more from advocacy and push toward serving a need.

"We will continue to be a catalyst and a resource driving change for folks that aren't there yet, and we will still be there to help those who have made the decision to join the effort."

Myron Marsh, President – CEO, Thomson-Shore, Inc.

"I think we have a lot of room to improve in the industry. I believe that the recycled content of books is somewhere around the five to six percent range. That is where Thomson-Shore was in 2004 before we signed the Green Press Initiative. In just two years, we have achieved over 25% recycled content. Through year to date in 2007 after the first quarter, we are at 38%. That is a huge amount of improvement. Last year that equates to something like one and a quarter million pounds of recycled fiber that went out in books out of this facility. If I think that all of the other book manufacturers are somewhere in the five to six percent range and if we start moving everybody else up, that is going to have a tremendous impact industry-wide. So my vision is to see that. The Book Industry Treatise on Responsible Paper Use that we signed said that we would be part of encouraging the entire industry to get to 30% by 2011. This is my vision for the industry. My vision for Thomson-Shore is that we are a leading part of that effort."

Stephen F. Quill, Chairman – Ecological Fibers, Inc.

"The vision for Ecological Fibers is that it will continue to look for ways that ensure using green components, or my terminology, 'environmentally sound components'. We constantly look for better ways. We believe in an open door policy with our suppliers. If they come up with an environmentally sound product, we want to be the first ones they come tell about it. On an international basis the developed societies like our own, Europe, and other developed countries are further along in having the ability to produce products that are green than some of the under developed countries.

"The question comes back to the people who buy the products. We sell to three different distinct groups of people: book publishing, office products, and then packaging including special types of packaging and security documents. If those people buy into 'green' publishing, it's great. It will come forward a lot faster than someone saying, 'I do it this way because it was the way they did it thirty years ago.'

"In our case we have spent a lot of time learning how to do the things that we have been discussing. We have got a lot of blood, sweat, tears and money in developing them. Would we share those with everybody? Well, we certainly can tell them that it can be done. In the last fifteen years, there has been a major change in our industry. Suppliers are interested in producing green products, when and where they can.

"I think society will demand it. It is a matter of buyers insisting that their suppliers provide green products whenever possible. You want them to hear that green is important to you—then it will happen."

Deborah Bruner, Director, Book Publishing Papers, New Leaf Paper

"The biggest thing is just thinking beyond the U.S., thinking beyond North America. When I founded the AAUP Eco Task Force, one of the first things we started discussing was how publishing and the paper and printing industries in North America compare with those abroad. In the United States and Canada, you have a lot of publishers getting on board with using recycled paper. They are becoming aware of forestry issues and are cognizant that old growth trees should not be harvested for toilet paper, or for their books for that matter. As we ask our North American printers and paper suppliers to 'do the right thing'—whether it is to use environmentally friendly inks to recycled paper or to not cut old growth forests—we need to make sure we don't turn a blind eye to what is happening elsewhere around the world. Publishing, printing, and paper manufacturing is a global marketplace. It's important to educate ourselves about illegal logging in parts of Indonesia and Russia, or pulp mill pollution in China where clean drinking water is becoming harder and harder to find. Much of the paper purchased for books can be sourced to environmental degradation around the world. Our biggest challenge is to make sure everybody, everywhere, is on the same page when it comes to pursuing eco-friendly options. Companies in all parts of the world need to hear the same message and be accountable to the same standards. Some publishers are guilty of asking their North American suppliers to be eco-friendly, while turning a blind eye to counterparts in Asia.

"My vision of 'green' publishing is to take the good things that are happening in the U.S. and Canada abroad to prevent whatever disasters are brewing, especially in places like China, just to prevent them before they get any worse than they already are."

Tony Crouch, Director, Design & Production, University of California Press

"For University of California Press it will hopefully be more of the same. In the last two years, we have expanded the use of green papers from the text papers into paperback-cover stocks and to the dust-jacket papers as well. We worked with our component printers to get them on board and to agree to stock those kinds of materials for the paperback covers and dust jackets. They weren't previously using that kind of material, but now they are. I have tried to help them by asking for the support of other university presses to join with us in specifying these materials. This encourages the printer to order them in economically viable quantities. So, as long as I am here, it will be more of the same — and hopefully — ever-increasing more of the same. I don't intend to just let it lie. We can honestly say we try to make our books environmentally responsible and 'green' from cover to cover."

Margo Baldwin, President and Publisher, Chelsea Green Publishing Company

"We are trying to set the agenda which is difficult if you're pretty much a tiny company like us compared to the big, big players in the industry. In general, there is a lot more awareness about the issue of global warming, so we are showcasing how this can be done. We have launched a green partnership program with bookstores where we are trying to get them to commit to going non-returnable, which means all sales would be final. We are also encouraging them to have a green living sustainability display once a year, and we have volunteered to actually offset the shipping. We are going to ship to them free and offer a carbon offset for the shipping. So if this works, we can put this in front of the industry. I think it is a good model.

"A lot of people don't know this, but in the book business, nothing is sold until it is sold to the end customer. Generally speaking, stores that order your books can return them for full credit if they don't sell. So there is a tremendous amount of shipping of books back and forth. In fact, the overall percentage of returns for the trade probably runs around 40% or 50%. So there is just a huge amount of energy wasted shipping them back and forth for no reason since books are heavy. There is a lot of resistance on the part of the big players to go non-returnable because it means they can't put their books out in large quantities. The traditional strategy has been 'Ship as many out as you can, and then take about half of them back.' We want to basically minimize this to the extent possible.

"The way most retail industries work is that when you sell a product to a store, if the product doesn't sell, it is up to the store to mark it down and sell it off as a sale item. But you have actually sold it. In the book industry, you can sell a product out and if it doesn't sell, it just comes back to you. The bottom line on this is to change the industry to be more similar to other retail industries and just have a final sale. This mainly has to do with bookstores because if we sell to gardening stores or hardware stores or other kinds of retail outlets, we sell on a non-returnable basis and there's not a problem.

"In the *Publishers' Weekly* article, 'Zero-Waste Publishing' from August 14, 2006, that I wrote, I summed it up this way: 'The future is green. (It's the new fiscal black.) ... We are in the midst of formulating a new, nonreturnable sales strategy and invite booksellers and publishers who agree with us to join as partners in this effort. Not only is it the *virtuous* thing to do, it's the only *economic* thing to do.'

"In the more distant future digital publishing could become the venue where there is no paper and might become a lot more important. In this case, people would have electronic readers of some kind and you wouldn't be producing anything on paper. So I suppose that in the future that's one way to go, although the manufacturing of electronics is a fairly dirty process too. The net probably in terms of a person being able to have all their books on one electronic device: this would have less impact than printing paper and cutting down trees. In the distant future, that may be what happens."

Archie J. Beaton, Executive Director - CEO, Chlorine Free Products Association

"As for the future of 'green' publishing, we are trying to make it simple and easy. As a producer of pulp and paper, there is no more stringent and easy-to-understand guideline than what we offer. As a publisher, it is simple to adopt the SMI (Sustainable Manufacturing Initiative) certification guidelines that we have, just as the United Nations has done. In fact, the United Nations has this in their procurement guidelines: Supply of 100% processed chlorine-free recycled paper (CFPA certified)- Int- Ref-RQS_Nll4OO/NJL-: either the supplier has been certified as processed chlorine free under the CFPA guidelines or they don't procure the paper from them. We make it easy to have a tremendous impact that is measurable as third-party accountability for the industry.

"The United Nations has been doing this now since 1998, and they have been fairly successful. It has been quite amazing that every two years we get calls from paper companies that say, 'We want to get certified so that we can sell paper to the United Nations.' Each year we have to review what they say. When they read our guidelines and don't meet them, they basically drop out. They say they can't meet the criteria. We believe that in order to really be green, you have to have stringent guidelines."

Tom Kemper, CEO & Founder, Dolphin Blue

"Where Dolphin Blue really fits that picture of the future more than anything is our ability to provide publishing grades of paper that would be utilized more in the micro publishing arena as opposed to what most people think of when you say publishing. We are able to provide papers for the micro publishing sector and for individuals, anybody printing anything. I would love it if authors came to Dolphin Blue and said, 'You know, I'm writing my manuscript, and I am drafting my thoughts. I am getting it together for the publisher, and I want to produce all those pages that I am going to be producing on environmentally responsible paper.' So for that purpose we have 100% post consumer recycled and certified processed chlorine free copier, laser and inkjet printer paper. These papers can be put through laser printers or inkjet printers all day long. They can write on it, and it is just as beautiful as a non-recycled sheet. As consumers and businesses, we all have a huge opportunity to take a step in a positive environmental direction, not just for us but for future generations.

"Publishers and book authors often don't really look at their book as a business. When their book is a business, their business cards and the audio CD's that promote their book ideas can support the 'green' approach by being printed on 100% post-consumer recycled and certified processed chlorine free paper.

"By having that little business card or CD sleeve sample that is 100% post-consumer recycled and certified processed chlorine free, the author really has the ability to convey to the reader, or, with whomever they do business, the importance of environmentally responsible steps in their everyday life."

The vision of the future of "green" publishing has varying perspectives from our Collective Wisdom Team™. We honor all of them and look forward to the continuing progress ahead.

> **ESP Tip**™ ~ *The "green" book publishing industry continues to progress with new innovations and new efforts worldwide. The future is in your heart and the vision of book publishing is in your hands. Without you and your book, the future will never become a reality. So keep apprised of new happenings in the "green" book industry and ask for more information about the latest developments when producing your book.*

> **PAT Tip**™ ~ *Please keep writing and producing your books. Inform and educate your publishing team on the latest developments in "green" book publishing. Proactively seek the newest information available every time you bring your book to press. Check out our Cool Environmental Companies and Organizations in the Resource section in the back of this book frequently to keep up to date.*

CHAPTER : 5

Easy Conversations to Have with a Publisher
Or as we like to say... ask
"How do you make THAT book 'green'?"™

With all of these resources now at your fingertips, we want to reveal the most effective methods for discussing the production of your book in an environmentally sound way. In other words, "How do you make THAT book 'green'?"™ Now, it is your turn.

Take the guide with you to your publisher, printer, book manufacturer or book consultant and start with these simple steps to make your project as "green" as you choose:

The Secret: A-S-K!

When you want more information about anything, the first step is to acknowledge that you do not know and need assistance. It is awareness. Maybe you had an interest in making your book "green" before reading this book—or perhaps you have been inspired by the information presented here by our Collective Wisdom Team™ and us, the Green Guide Girls™.

We encourage you as a first step to ask your publisher, book manufacturer, printer or book consultant if they are familiar with "green" book publishing options. You can share this guide with them and let them know you are interested in using environmentally sound processes in the production and printing of your book.

From Dollars and Cents to Dollars and Sense

If the publishing team you are working with expresses a concern about the costs of publishing your book using "green" resources, request that all numbers be quoted so you can see your options. In many cases, the difference may result in a few pennies more per book. However, the overall cost to the planet may be worth it for you.

Be Specific

Use the information in Chapter 2 of this guide to review each component of the manufacturing process including the cover materials and endpapers (if applicable), the paper and ink for your book. Here is a quick reminder from Tyson Miller of the Green Press Initiative for your paper checklist:

"The Green Press Initiative has developed environmental standards that will enable authors and publishers to help the industry to reduce its environmental impacts within the existing supply infrastructure. The following are suggested guidelines:

1. Postconsumer Content
Minimum: 30% postconsumer recycled fiber content.

2. Virgin Fiber and/or Alternative Fiber Content
If a book is not printed on 100% postconsumer recycled paper, then it is recommended that, in addition to the minimum level of postconsumer recycled fiber, that the remaining fiber be drawn from one of the following categories:

• FSC (Forest Stewardship Council) certified fiber
• Preconsumer recycled fiber
• Non-wood fiber including but not limited to
(agricultural by-products, kenaf, hemp, or other)

3. Bleaching Process
It is recommended that book papers be bleached Processed Chlorine Free (PCF)."

~ Tyson Miller,
Director, Green Press Initiative

Let This Reference Be Your Guide

This book is chock-full of information to assist you with each step of your "green" publishing process. It is designed for easy reference during any publishing meeting. It is small so you can take it with you in your briefcase, tote bag or backpack.

We encourage you to refer to the information included here and to seek out updates on all of the websites of the Resources we have included for you in the back of the book.

To keep apprised of the most current certification information, please refer to the organizations and their respective websites in the Certifications section in the back of this guide.

Our Collective Wisdom Team™ is your team.
They along with all the resources mentioned
are prepared to assist you in making your book
as "green" as can be and as ecologically sound
as your heart desires.

ESP Tip™ ~ *Green is a magical color. When you make your book "green", you not only save the planet — you save society from the exorbitant costs for healthcare and wasted energy and materials. Most of all, your friends will be "green" with envy when they find out your book is eco-friendly. Cheer them on and show them the guide from the Green Guide Girls™! Let them know it is simple for anybody to make a book "green."*

PAT Tip™ ~ *Please get your book done and go on an eco-holiday!*

You have the power.

You have the information.

You have the contacts and websites.

All your questions can be answered.

All you have to do is—ask.

Epilogue

Everyone benefits from your book in ways they may never even realize when you use "green" book publishing resources.

Congratulations!

We are so thrilled that you now have the tools and information to make your book "green".

We look forward to hearing how easy it is for you to put on pigtails, raise your hand, and ask your championship publishing team, "How do I make THAT book 'green'?"™ Please email us at info@greenguidegirls.com and let us know about your "green" book publishing successes.

We encourage you to contact the resources provided in this book and ask them to help you, mentor you, and guide you to completion with a book that is produced with a sound approach. It is important to us that you ask, ask, ask so you have every opportunity to make your book "green, green, green".

We will continue to work with our Collective Wisdom Team™ to develop and support new ideas to grow the "green" book publishing industry for you.

We have fallen in love with this project and see its impact already. We as the Green Guide Girls™ feel that you have the opportunity to lead the way—since the book publishing industry does not exist without your creativity, ideas and desire to print books. We encourage you to make an educated decision in this moment to choose to use ecologically sound practices to change the world.

Thank you for makin' it easy to be "green".

Be well and prosper green.

Warmly with respect and gratitude,

Cindy Katz   Jennifer S. Wilkov

The Green Guide Girls™

The Green Guide Girls™
We ask the question:
"How do you make THAT 'green'?"™

Our mission:
Through quick information
and simple steps,
we help people learn that it's easy
to make anything "green".

www.greenguidegirls.com

ACKNOWLEDGMENTS

Appreciation and acknowledgments are an important part of the book publishing process and the foundation for meaningful sustainable relationships. It is one of the most important sections of the book which requires careful consideration, thoughtful "thank you's," and a major pat on the back for those who have put up with the outrageous effort we put forth to make this book happen. It is truly an all consuming process.

Books do not come to life overnight, even though this particular book feels like it did. Our cute, little joy-filled guide would not be possible without these individuals and companies.

There are many people in our mutual and respective lives that have supported us through this amazing journey. You see, this little book was produced and published in less than ninety days. It was a Herculean effort to complete because we were given a surprise invitation to provide it for all the university presses at their annual AAUP meeting in 2007. We took on the challenge to meet this date—and everyone on the book publishing team rose to this occasion to make miracles happen for us.

We felt the timing of our work was universally aligned with all the "green" activities and concerns being discussed in our society and the book publishing world. We have approached this project thoughtfully and courageously to make this book happen as quickly as possible—to serve the demand for it in the book publishing industry and to bring greater attention to the environmental considerations of the book business. We want to thank everyone for recognizing that it is not necessarily perfection that is important to us. We are always perfectly learning and providing our work with our best efforts and to the highest of our abilities. The constant learning process is the true gift of the book project experience.

Together, we would like to thank the following from the bottom of our little pigtail hearts:

Our mentors and friends in the book publishing and "green" worlds have encouraged and inspired our work together. We want to thank Mark Victor Hansen, Robert G. Allen, Larry Kirshbaum, Graham Hill and Ken Rother, and Jack Canfield.

Daniel Katz has been incredibly supportive for us, as both food preparer and general technical support. He has provided for our mutual comfort, nourishment, and connectivity. He created a magical working environment for us by making it possible for the Katz children to enjoy this writing process with us without feeling like their mommy was missing from their everyday lives. Thank you, Danny, from the bottom of our little Green Guide Girl™ hearts.

The book production team is an amazing group of individuals and companies that chose to support our work in so many ways: moral support, guidance on the "green" aspects of our book, the rush printing job completed to make sure that we made it to the university press conference, and beyond.

A big thank you to Billy Kelly of YAY! Design, our amazing cover designer and an outstanding musician; Craig P. Cardone, our interior text designer, and Debbie Ann Schneider, an amazing friend and top-notch researcher; and Susie Ward of The Admin Source for her great contributions and support for this project — our files would have never made it to the printer without you!

Thank you to Mark A. Hicks for the image of the Green Guide Girls™, that inspires our simple pigtail approach. We appreciate your generosity — and you.

Thank you to John Sinclair, Justin McLean, Dave Raymond and the whole team at Thomson-Shore, Inc., for printing and manufacturing this book using soy-based ink on 100% PCR Rolland Enviro100 paper. This paper contains 100% post-consumer fiber; is certified "Ecologo", "Processed Chlorine Free" and "FSC Recycled"; and is manufactured using biogas energy.

Tom Rohlfing, Roger Wissmann, and the entire team at Pinnacle Press produced the covers on 100% PCW Sakura 100 paper, which is certified Processed Chlorine Free, manufactured with Green-e® certified wind power, and designated Ancient Forest Friendly. We also want to thank Deborah Bruner at New Leaf Paper for stewarding the paper selection for the cover with us.

We want to single out Steve Bedney of the Ecological Fibers team, who was the first person we spoke with about this project. It was his direction to several people that set us off on our journey through the "green" book publishing world. Thank you, Steve, for being a big supporter of our work and project.

We reached out into the book publishing world and those who have acknowledged their participation in the "green" efforts within the industry. We want to thank the following companies for opening and answering our mass email request for participation in this little "green" guide: Baker Publishing Group, Book Publishing Company, Council Oak Books, Four Way Books, GBL & CLjr Publishing, Good Spirited Company, Hampton Roads Publishing Company, Harvard University Press, Impact Publishers Inc., Kedzie Press, Leaping Dog Press/ Asylum Arts Press, Nomad Press and Dogtooth Books, Pruett Publishing, Silver Light Publications, Dirigo Paper Mills, Grays Harbor Paper, Myllykoski North America, McNaughton & Gunn, New Society Publishers, Environmental Paper Network, Fidlar Doubleday, and Raincoast Books.

Now, we want to turn our attention to an amazing group of individuals whom we would like to acknowledge and offer our warmest, deepest gratitude: our Collective Wisdom Team™. Each person makes an incredible effort to assist authors, publishers, book manufacturers, and printers with their books. Through this project, we have been able to add the credit of "writer" to their resume by having them provide their stories, insights, knowledge, wisdom and experience throughout the book. Here they are—our beloved friends and mentors of the Green Guide Girls'™ Collective Wisdom Team™:

Tom Kemper, CEO & Founder, Dolphin Blue: Tom was one of the first people we spoke with about this project. We greatly appreciate his deep love for and abiding commitment to the environment and us. Tom dearly wants us to succeed at this, as he says that our "heart" is in the right place. Thanks, Tom, for your knowledge, special care, and passion to achieve sustainability. Thank you for always being happy to assist in every way you are able.

Tyson Miller, Director, Green Press Initiative: Tyson is a phenomenal human being who cares deeply about the health of Planet Earth. We commend and support his efforts through

GPI. We want to thank you, Tyson, for your never-ending support and the beautiful foreword you provided for us for this book. Thank you so much for being who you are.

Stephen F. Quill, Chairman—Ecological Fibers, Inc.: Steve is one of our role models and all around exemplary human beings. His dedication to his family, business, employees and the environment is outstanding. We have learned so much from him in such a short period of time. Thank you, Steve, for your generous spirit and trust and confidence in our work as the Green Guide Girls™. You are one of our heroes.

Myron Marsh, President-CEO, Thomson-Shore, Inc.: Myron has quickly become a dear friend and supporter of our efforts as the Green Guide Girls™. He stewards a company filled with warm and wonderful workers who, like him, are dedicated to the highest quality service, environmentally responsible book manufacturing, and education of any and all members of the publishing community. Thank you, Myron, for treating us with kindness, respect and love during our project and for inviting us up to the Thomson-Shore world any time we want to tap into it.

Archie J. Beaton, Executive Director-CEO, Chlorine Free Products Association: Archie is kind, articulate, passionate, and committed to a healthier planet filled with designs for a sustainable future. He is dedicated to informing children of all ages of the value of eliminating harmful chemicals from major water supply sources. From our early morning meetings, phone calls and emails, to his gentle way of explaining complex terminology to us simply and elegantly, Archie is a beacon of light in the "green" book publishing community. We appreciate you, Archie, for everything that you believe in and stand up for every day.

Tony Crouch, Director, Design & Production, University of California Press: Tony is an insightful, supportive and passionate person in the "green" book publishing world. Through his single-handed efforts, he inspires us and his colleagues to continue to make groundbreaking progress in the book publishing industry. His efforts with the Association of American University Presses led to our first opportunity to get this guide out into the book publishing world in a big way. Thank you, Tony, for being a giant supporter of our work as the Green Guide Girls™. We respect and admire your continuing contributions to the industry. You light up our world.

Deborah Bruner, Director, Book Publishing Papers, New Leaf Paper: Deb cares so deeply about the education and welfare of her clients — and the earth. She has been incredibly kind and generous with her time, energy and efforts to debunk much of the paper mysteries we encountered during this project. From her early dedication to environmental issues to her integrity-based work at New Leaf Paper, Deb has welcomed our questions, confusion and last minute content approvals with elegance, grace and loving support. Thank you, Deb, for being so kind to us. We look forward to our continuing long-lasting relationship filled with our combined efforts to benefit our respective companies and the planet.

Margo Baldwin, President and Publisher, Chelsea Green Publishing Company: Margo is a generous, warm and passionate person who, along with her husband, has dedicated her work to "green" book publishing. Since 1984, she has committed herself to providing thoughtful, innovative and practical solutions to the industry as a whole. Her approach to book publishing is exemplary, and her desire to inform and educate is inspiring. Thank you, Margo, for the lessons we learned with you during this process.

There is one company that we would also like to mention here. SKYPE™ (Skype Limited) has contributed significantly to our enjoyment of writing this book. With one of us in New Jersey and the other in New York, it could have been a challenge to write together. With its crazy little icons and our ability to "barf" on each other, clap and cheer each other on, celebrate with a party hat, giggle, or send each other a smiling ray of sunshine, a big smile, a big red beating heart and a growing flower, SKYPE™ made our writing efforts effortless and fun.

Cindy is thankful for her blessed life and wants to personally thank the following people:

Thank you to my family, all of them, as the family tree is where I come from. My family roots brought the water to sustain me as I grew up.

Thank you, Mom, Arlene Mersten, for reading the text—you were the first one!

I especially appreciate and adore Danny and the kids for their love and support and for bringing me food and kisses when I was upstairs in my room, on the computer and on the phone, working on my Green Guide Girls™ "school project". You are what my life is all about: sunshine. Thank you for being my teachers, all of you.

A very special "Todah" to our friends Dani and Sari, for bringing a divine secret to our family's life to enable us to reach this point.

Thank you to the entire magical Dream Tree Team at Plant a Tree USA™, especially Donna Hook, Bella Parcell, and Danny Verbov, for their devotion, dedication, warmth, love, and care.

A special thank you to John C. Miller, III Esq., my legal counsel, for your support in all my ventures and adventures. You protect me with care and expertise. Thank you to Vicki Bosler, my Quickbooks assistant for her expertise, understanding, and down-to-earth manner. Thank you to Geoff Smith at SCORE, my "boss".

Thank you, Clinton Swaine, the master of experiential games, for our life-changing "hikes" and "jumps" into waterfalls and to our Mastermind teams. I also thank Chip Collins for his savvy sales mentoring and caring support.

A special thank you to Jennifer S. Wilkov, award-winning partner and best-selling writer, for her transparency, coaching, professional support, and for enjoying each other as we create and "SKYPE™" and make bold moves, based in deep ethics and love, to change today for a better greener tomorrow. I had no idea how meaningful this process was ... Thank you, Jennifer, for going through it with me!

Jennifer would also like to personally acknowledge the following people who assist and support her with the life she wants to live:

I want to thank my extraordinary family including my mother, Marjorie Wilkov, and her beau, Tim Moehnke; my father, Howard Wilkov, and his wife, Betty; my beloved brother, Jeffrey Wilkov, and his beautiful wife, Kristina, and their children, my blessed nieces, Sydney Rachel and Logan Porter; my amazing and inspirational grandmother, Charlotte Hillsberg; and all of my extended family members. Sometimes they don't quite understand what I do as an author until they hold the book in their hands. Yet, they are always my biggest supporters and cheerleaders. May this book help each of them realize that a book really can be a full-time job and business with a clear purpose and income stream while providing a valuable service to humankind and the planet.

I want to thank my beloved friends inside and outside of the book publishing industry who continue to support my work, my dreams and the choices I make to live the life I want to live: Krisha Marcano from Theater Chicks Productions; Manny Goldman from PersonalGrowth.com; Rabbi Linda and David Shriner-Cahn; John Willig; Larry Kirshbaum; Robert G. Allen; Helen Deitelzweig; Lord Phillip and Bianca Wren and their beautiful family; Dennis R. Miller, CFP®, and everyone who has touched my heart and soul with their kind words and loving support.

Thank you to a special gentleman who has stood by me through the biggest learning period of my life. David Halperin of Halperin & Halperin, P.C.: I am so grateful for you—my true Guardian Angel, legal advisor and business team strategist. Thank you for believing in me. I love you and feel so blessed to have you in my life and on my personal championship team.

Special thanks also to my intellectual property team, Ross Charap and Myka Todman at Moses & Singer LLP, for standing by me and supporting my publishing pursuits with their unique legal acumen.

I love to learn and enlist the teachings and support of my own mentors who have become personal friends. Thank you to all, both living and those who influence me by the lives they led, for sharing your insights, knowledge, wisdom and guidance with me: Keith Cunningham, Albert Einstein, Benjamin Franklin, R. Buckminster Fuller, Norman Vincent Peale, Walt Disney, Anthony Robbins, T. Harv Eker, Joel and Heidi Roberts, Sarah Singer-Nourie, M.A.; Jay Abraham; Mother Theresa, Marie Curie, Helen Keller, Aunt Susan Horwitz, Ph.D.; Evance Steven Kiwelu; my beloved Shintaido senseis, H.F. Ito and Toshimitsu Ishii, and everyone in the worldwide Shintaido community; my blessed Aikido sensei, Don Cardoza, and everyone at the Wellness Resource Center and dojo in North Dartmouth, MA; and my grandparents, Philip S. Hillsberg and Fay and Al Wilkov, who have passed on in life yet still inspire me with their amazing life stories.

As the publisher of E.S.P. Press Corp., I want to thank my amazing championship team including Debbi Whiting, my beloved personal assistant and shipping maven, the wonderful distribution team at Midpoint Trade Books, and the loving support and guidance from everyone who has helped me succeed in the book publishing industry.

There is one person whom I feel privileged to have in my life. Cindy Katz, who I affectionately call Mama Katz, is an amazing human being. Being the mother of five beautiful children, sustaining a fulfilling inspirational marriage, running a business and stewarding her professional team, and being my beloved writing partner in the Green Guide Girls™ adventures — somehow she manages to make every person in her life feel loved, supported and complete. Cindy always has more than enough love for everyone she meets and every tree on the planet. She is an integral part of my joy with the Green Guide Girls™ activities, and I am so grateful that she asked me to be her partner in this amazing journey. Thank you, Cindy Mindy, from the tips of my toes to the depths of my "wittle" Green Guide Girl™ soul for being my partner and blessed friend.

Almighty God is a thriving force in our mutual lives. We would like to take this moment to be grateful for the divine inspiration and commandments, loving guidance, and spiritual support we find in the teachings of the Torah and our religious practices. In the words of an inspiring song of praise attributed to one of the greatest early liturgical poets who flourished during the 11th century, we respect and thank the "Master of the universe, Who reigned before any form was created."

We see everything that we do
as a blessing, our responsibility
while here on Earth.

Finally, we would like to acknowledge you, the reader, for taking the time and having the interest to read what we have put together in this cute, fun-filled, information-packed book. Without you, we cannot fulfill our personal missions of being successful in business in conjunction with doing our part to honor, respect and preserve the beautiful planet we live on. We send you pigtailed thank you's and a warm hug for embracing our work and considering the thoughtful information provided here for your book projects.

Book publishing is a great gift.
We feel blessed to share this "green" book
with you.

RESOURCE SECTION

Who's Who in Green Book Publishing

🐝 indicates a member of the Green Guide Girls'™
Collective Wisdom Team™

Publishers

Baker Publishing Group
Website: www.bakerpublishinggroup.com
Phone: 1-616-676-9185

Book Publishing Company
Website: www.bookpubco.com
Email: info@bookpubco.com
Phone: 1-888-260-8458

Chelsea Green Publishing Company 🐝
Website: www.chelseagreen.com
Email: mbaldwin@chelseagreen.com
Phone: 1-802-295-6300
"The politics & practice of sustainable living"

Council Oak Books

Website: www.counciloakbooks.com
Email: publicity@counciloakbooks.com
Phone: 1-800-247-8850

E.S.P. Press Corp.

Website: www.GetMyESPPress.com
Email: Jennifer@GetMyESP.com
Phone: 1-718-797-7600 x12
From Thought to Sales in 90 Days™
"Turn your idea into a book, and your book into a thriving business."™

Four Way Books

Website: www.fourwaybooks.com
Email: four_way_editors@yahoo.com
Phone: 1-800-421-1561

GBL & CLjr Publishing

Website: www.gopopsi.com
Email: recycle@gopopsi.com

Good Spirited Company

Website: www.goodspirited.com
Email: news@goodspirited.com

Hampton Roads Publishing Company

Website: www.hrpub.com
Phone: 1-434-296-2772

Harvard University Press
Website: www.hup.harvard.edu
Email: Contact_HUP@harvard.edu
Phone: 1-800-406-9145

Impact Publishers, Inc.
Website: www.impactpublishers.com
Email: publisher@impactpublishers.com
Phone: 1-805-466-5917

Kedzie Press
Website: www.kedziepress.com
Email: jessicasanchez@kedziepress.com
Phone: 1-877-550-1960

Leaping Dog Press / Asylum Arts Press
Website: www.leapingdogpress.com
Email: editor@leapingdogpress.com

Nomad Press and Dogtooth Books
Website: www.nomad-press.com
Email: nomad@nomad-press.com
Phone: 1-970-226-3590

Pruett Publishing
Website: www.pruettpublishing.com
Email: info@pruettpublishing.com
Phone: 1-303-449-4919

Silver Light Publications
Website: www.silverlightpub.com
Email: info@silverlightpub.com
Phone: 1-541-552-1061

University of California Press

Website: www.ucpress.edu
Email: askucp@ucpress.edu
Phone: 1-510-642-4247

Paper

Dirigo Paper Mills

Website: www.dirigopaper.com
Email: DKLAM@DirigoPaper.com
Phone: 1-802-892-6100

Grays Harbor Paper

Website: www.ghplp.com
Email: dquigg@ghplp.com
Phone: 1-877-548-3424

Mohawk Fine Papers

Website: www.mohawkpaper.com
Phone: 1-800-THE MILL (1-800-843-6455)

Myllykoski North America

Website: www.myllykoski.com
Email: myllykoski.paper@myllykoski.com
Phone: 1-203 229-7417

Neenah Paper

Website: www.neenahpaper.com

New Leaf Paper ఴఴ
Website: www.newleafpaper.com
Email: info@newleafpaper.com
Phone: 1-888-989-5323
Bringing you beautiful papers through environmental innovation.

Paper Distributors

Dolphin Blue ఴఴ
Website: www.dolphinblue.com
Email: query@dolphinblue.com
Phone: 1-800-932-7715
Environmentally responsible office supplies for a sustainable world

Printers

Fidlar Doubleday
Website: www.fidlardoubleday.com
Email: info@fidlar-doubleday.com
Phone: 1-800-248-0888

Integrated Book Technology (IBT or IBT Global)
Website: www.integratedbook.com
Email: general@integratedbook.com
Phone: 1-518-271-5117
Digital printing; Books manufactured on-demand (POD)

Thomson-Shore, Inc.
Website: www.tshore.com
Email: questions@tshore.com
Phone: 1-734-426-3939
Book manufacturer, Printer, Strategic partner for publishers,
Reputation for doing the job right the first time.

Pinnacle Press, Inc.
Website: www.pinnaclepress.com
Email: tom@pinnaclepress.com
Phone: 1-800-760-0010
Color Printer, Book Component Printer, Cover and Jacket
Printer

Cover Materials

Dirigo Paper Mills
Website: www.dirigopapers.com
Email: DKLAM@DirigoPaper.com
Phone: 1-802-892-6100

Ecological Fibers, Inc.
Website: www.ecofibers.com
Email: info@ecofibers.com
Phone: 1-978-537-0003
Environmentally sound cover solutions

Endpapers

Dirigo Paper Mills
Website: www.dirigopapers.com
Email: DKLAM@DirigoPaper.com
Phone: 1-802-892-6100

Rainbow®
Website: www.ecofibers.com
Email: info@ecofibers.com
Phone: 1-978-537-0003
Environmentally sound cover solutions

Book Manufacturers

Integrated Book Technology (IBT or IBT Global)
Website: www.integratedbook.com
Email: general@integratedbook.com
Phone: 1-518-271-5117
Digital printing; Books manufactured on-demand (POD)

McNaughton & Gunn
Website: www.bookprinters.com
Phone: 1-734-429-5411

Thomson-Shore, Inc.
Website: www.tshore.com
Email: questions@tshore.com
Phone: 1-734-426-3939
Book manufacturer, Printer, Strategic partner for publishers
Reputation for doing the job right the first time.

Book Consultants

E.S.P. Press Corp.
Website: www.GetMyESPPress.com
Email: Jennifer@GetMyESP.com
Phone: 1-718-797-7600 x12
From Thought to Sales in 90 Days™
"Turn your idea into a book, and your book into a thriving business."™

Other Cool Environmental Companies and Organizations

Environmental Defense
Website: www.environmentaldefense.org
Email: members@environmentaldefense.org
Phone: 1-800-684-3322

Environmental Paper Network
Website: www.environmentalpaper.org
Email: joshua@environmentalpaper.org
Phone: 1-828-251-8558

Environmental Protection Agency
Website: www.epa.gov

Forest Ethics
Website: www.forestethics.org
Email: info@forestethics.org
Phone: 1-415-863-4563

Green Press Initiative

Website: www.greenpressinitiative.com
Email: tyson@greenpressinitiative.org
Phone: 1-828-994-0859
Leader in environmentally responsible book publishing advocacy

Plant a Tree USA™

Website: www.plantatreeusa.com
Website: www.authorssaveworld.com
Email: trees@plantatreeusa.com
Phone: 1-877-A-Tree-4-U
Authors Save World™ program, to educate and encourage tree plantings through books.

Treehugger

Website: www.treehugger.com
Email: info@treehugger.com   .
TreeHugger is the leading online media company dedicated to everything modern and green. Offering environmental news, product information, and tools to help people green their lives, TreeHugger is helping to propel sustainability into the mainstream.

Canadian Sources

Cascades Fine Paper Group

Website: www.environmentalbychoice.com
Email: infofinepapers@cascades.com
Phone: From Canada 1-800-567-9872
        From USA 1-800-388-0882

Environment Canada

Website: www.ec.gc.ca
Email: enviroinfo@ec.gc.ca
Phone: From Canada 1-800-668-6767
From USA 1-819-997-2800

Markets Initiative

Website: www.marketsinitiative.org
Email: marketsinitiative@marketsinitiative.org
Phone: 1-604-253-7701 x23

New Society Publishers

Website: www.newsociety.com
Email: info@newsociety.com
Phone: 1-250-247-9737

Raincoast Books

Website: www.raincoast.com
Email: info@raincoast.com
Phone: 1-604-323-7100

Green Certifications

Chlorine Free Products Association

Website: www.chlorinefreeproducts.org
Email: info@chlorinefreeproducts.org
Phone: 1-847-658-6104
Chlorine bleaches out Life.

Green-e® Certified Renewable Energy

Website: www.green-e.org
Email: info@green-e.org
Phone: 1-415-561-2100

Forest Stewardship Council
Website: www.fsc.org
Email: ndaly@fscus.org
Phone: 1-202-342-0413

Calculators

Website: www.AreYouUpATree.com
Calculator estimates how many trees to plant to offset your
carbon pollution by the travel and energy you use when
creating and marketing your book. Created by Plant a Tree
USA™. Scientific research provided by the Environmental
Protection Agency and the US Department of Transportation.

Website: www.papercalculator.org
Estimate environmental impacts, using the Environmental
Defense Paper Calculator.

This book went from thought to print in less than 90 days.

There are additional companies and organizations
which have not yet responded to us and our inquiry
about their green resources. We are happy to include all
green-conscious book publishing world resources.

To be in our next edition or to suggest that
someone be in our next edition
or to be a guest on our radio show,
please contact us info@greenguidegirls.com

G-L-O-S-S-A-R-Y

**Green Loving Outstanding Simple Succinct
Alphabetical Responsible Yippee**

~~~~~~

The purpose of this section is to debunk the "green" lingo that scares many people from asking about "green" options!

Our glossary is written for you to "get it." We thank you for reading through this glossary, a book section usually kept only as a reference.

In this case, you will find a warm introduction to some new words and ideas, a spin on some familiar terms, and our "cheat sheet" to help you enter into and be part of a dialogue.

No one needs to understand every term perfectly ... we encourage you to smile, nod your head, and say, "Wow! – It is easy to understand 'green'".

Acid-free ~ a term which is neither eco-friendly nor eco-harmful. It simply describes the chemistry of the paper. This is important when considering non-yellowing of the paper over its lifetime. Often acid-free paper can last for hundreds of years!

Bleaching ~ the whitening of paper. This is a process that often uses chlorine, which harms the environment.

Carbon offset ~ an environmental action step to "balance out" or "make up for" carbon pollution, i.e.: planting trees and using renewable energy.

Chlorine ~ a chemical dangerous to humans and other species. It pollutes our waterways.

Chlorine-free ~ a designation for paper that is manufactured without chlorine in the bleaching process.

Clear cutting ~ a method by which all or most of the trees in a given area are cut down. Many times, this method is associated with little or no environmental regeneration plan for the land.

Collective Wisdom Team™ ~ top leaders in the "green" book publishing world who are the beloved advisory group for the Green Guide Girls™.

De-inking ~ the process of removing "applied inks, finishes, glues, and other contaminants from wastepaper in order to extract the cellulose fiber" (New Leaf Paper website, www.newleafpaper.com). This is a necessary and extensive process that occurs during the production of recycled paper.

"Eco-llaboration" ~ a blending of "the art of writing" and "the science of manufacturing", synthesized with ecologically sound practices. A Green Guide Girls'™ term created during the writing of this book.

Eco-holiday ~ a vacation taken as a gift to yourself upon the completion of your "green" book.

Emissions ~ these are best explained as pollution coming from industry processes and transportation vehicle exhaust. Maximum amounts are regulated by the government, though ecologically sound individual companies have made great strides with their own initiatives to reduce the pollution levels they emit into the air.

ESP Tip™ ~ "Environmentally Sound Principle" provided by the Green Guide Girls™ at the end of each chapter of their books.

FSC ~ Forest Stewardship Council. An environmentally credible forest products certification and labeling program, "developed and defined by the conservation community" (Tyson Miller, Green Press Initiative).

Green ~ color used to describe things which are good for the environment, humans and fellow-earth species; ecologically conscious. (Cindy's favorite color, too!)

Green Guide Girls™ ~ two fun loving girls with pigtails, raising their hands and asking their simple question "How do we make THAT 'green'?"™

Logging ~ an industry and practice of cutting down trees to make wood products from trees.

Old growth forest ~ also known as Ancient Forest, this is an area which has not been disturbed by logging, clear-cutting, or development building.

Paper procurement ~ the act of purchasing or acquiring paper.

PAT Tip™ ~ "Please Act Today" action step provided by the Green Guide Girls™ at the end of each chapter of their books.

Percent (%) recycled paper ~ a mathematical description of how much of the paper comes from recycled materials.

Petroleum-based inks ~ these are made from fossil fuels. These inks pose threats to the environment: heavy metals get into our soil and groundwater, VOC's contribute to smog, and poisons and irritants degrade the health of print shop workers.

Post-consumer recycled (PCR) paper ~ made from post-consumer waste.

Post-consumer waste ~ "paper that has already been used and returned through a recycling program, thereby diverting it from a landfill or incinerator. It is usually de-inked and then processed to make new paper. Office paper waste makes up the majority of post-consumer waste content that is used to make recycled copy and printing papers." (New Leaf Paper website, www.newleafpaper.com)

100% Post-consumer recycled paper ~ the most environmentally friendly paper.

Pre-consumer recycled paper ~ made from pre-consumer waste.

Pre-consumer waste ~ materials that "have not met their intended end-use by a consumer and include allowable waste left over from manufacturing, converting, and printing processes. Examples: mill-converting scraps, pre-consumer de-inking material, pulp substitutes. Magazines and newspapers that were never bought also are termed pre-consumer." (New Leaf Paper website, www.newleafpaper.com)

Pulp ~ these are materials for making paper. They are manufactured from wood, recycled paper, and other materials.

Recycled paper ~ paper made with waste content. Please refer to both **post-consumer recycled paper** and **pre-consumer recycled paper** entries, in this G-L-O-S-S-A-R-Y.

Renewable energy ~ this is power that is made available using resources which can be replenished, such as wind, sun (solar-powered), and water (hydro-powered). These resources are "greener" than fossil fuels, as their use creates less pollution.

Sequester carbon ~ the process by which trees cleanse air from carbon pollution. Trees actually uptake carbon from the air (like "inhaling through their leaves") in order to photosynthesize and create oxygen for us to breathe. Plant a Tree USA™ affectionately refers to trees as "mean green carbon-reducing machines"™ due to their sequestering (uptake) of carbon pollution from the air.

SFI ~ Sustainable Forestry Initiative. This is a certification and labeling program backed by the forestry-industry. According to our trusted resources, this organization has been found to have lower standards of environmentally sound practices than FSC.

Solvent-based ~ a term often used when describing chemicals which are not environmentally sound. These are not water-based, which is the preferred method to be kind to the earth.

Soy based inks ~ an environmentally friendlier alternative to petroleum-based inks that are made from soybeans. These inks emit lower VOC's which decrease air pollution. It is easier for the recycling process when soy based inks are used. They create sharp bright colors. However, these inks have restrictions for use on certain printing presses. Soy based inks still contain a large percent of petroleum, but less than the petroleum-based inks. These inks are an example of part of the "green" spectrum where the industry is working to create products with lower ecological impact.

Sustainability ~ a lifestyle involving choices, balance, and systems to use and protect our resources wisely for humans and the earth, now and for the long-term.

Tree line ~ an ecological term describing the "edge" of a habitat beyond which trees can not grow due to the natural conditions which are not suitable for trees. This is a common picture at high altitudes at the point of transition from a view of trees to no trees.

Vegetable based inks ~ an environmentally friendlier alternative to both petroleum-based and soy-based inks. These emit less VOC's than both soy and petroleum-based inks. They have restrictions on certain printing presses.

Virgin paper ~ contains no recycled content.

Volatile Organic Compounds (VOC's) ~ these are chemicals which are harmful to humans and the earth. They contribute to air and water pollution when they escape into the air through evaporation.

Water-based ~ a term describing environmentally preferred alternatives over solvent-based chemicals.

Most of the terms have been defined with our own Green Guide Girls™ explanations.

Many of our Collective Wisdom Team™ members had a part in educating us so we could take the scientific gook out of the definition and provide you with terms that are memorable and easy to understand. Our specific thanks to the Green Press Initiative, New Leaf Paper, and the Chlorine Free Products Association for their support with this G-L-O-S-S-A-R-Y.

Note: Some research for these terms was completed using Wikipedia and Merriam-Webster online to facilitate the creation of this G-L-O-S-S-A-R-Y.

CERTIFICATIONS

There are many "green" certifications you may come across as you journey through the "green" book publishing world. Certifications exist to assure that what companies claim about their environmental responsibility is indeed verified. We have included a few common certifications including the logo and a brief description to make these symbols friendly and easy to understand.

Processed Chlorine Free (PCF) ~ reserved for recycled content paper. PCF papers have not been re-bleached with chlorine containing compounds.

Totally Chlorine Free (TCF) ~ reserved for virgin fiber papers. TCF papers do not use pulp produced with chlorine or chlorine containing compounds as bleaching agents.
(PCF and TCF descriptions, courtesy: Chlorine-Free Products Association, www.chlorinefreeproducts.org)

FSC

The Forest Stewardship Council (FSC) certification logo identifies paper whose virgin fiber comes from responsibly managed forests. FSC sets the highest standards for defining "responsible forest management," namely, forestry that is environmentally responsible, socially beneficial and economically viable. While the FSC focused on sustainable virgin fiber sources for most of its history, it recently began certifying papers with high post-consumer recycled content. The FSC requires certification from everyone in the supply chain—from logger to printer. One environmentally weak link in the chain and it's not FSC certified. (www.fsc.org)

Why Good Stewardship Matters: When you buy FSC certified products, you promote responsible forest management across the supply chain. The FSC is highly regarded because they developed these standards with everyone's input: not just environmental groups, but also logging companies, governments, indigenous peoples and labor.

ANCIENT FOREST
FRIENDLY

Ancient Forest Friendly™ (AFF) is a designation to get excited about, as it represents the most comprehensive standards for environmental responsibility in the paper industry. To earn the AFF designation, a paper must be manufactured with a high percentage of post-consumer waste and not contain any virgin fiber from old-growth, ancient or endangered forests. Any virgin fiber in the paper must be both FSC certified and assessed to not originate from endangered forests. Bleaching methods must be "chlorine free," meaning without the use of chlorine or chlorine compounds. To find out how you can use Ancient Forest Friendly™ paper and the logo, visit www.marketsinitiative.org

Why Protecting Ancient Forests Matters: Every day, ancient, old growth and endangered forests worldwide are being chopped down. It's more than the individual trees at stake—it's the forests, which are as critical to the world's climate as your lungs are to breathing. Once logged, forests with all their plants and wildlife can't simply be replanted. They're gone. When you use an Eco Audit for papers that are designated AFF, you reassure customers that you chose to spare these forests.

Green-e® Certified Renewable Energy ~ Green-e® is the nation's leading independent certification and verification program for renewable energy products in the U.S. The Green-e® logo is a nationally recognized symbol that identifies superior, certified renewable energy products. (www.green-e.org)

Why Clean Energy Matters: Environmental leadership extends beyond recycling. To reduce greenhouse gases and prevent climate change, we invest in energy credits that offset the energy needed to manufacture many of our papers. When you invest in paper made with wind power and biogas, you're helping to grow emission-free energy industries that will decrease our dependence on fossil fuels, reduce the emissions that cause global warming, and alleviate the air pollution that causes diseases such as asthma.

Biogas certification verifies that energy is sourced from the decomposition of waste, converting a waste stream and potent greenhouse gas into an energy source.
(FSC, AFF, Green-e, and Biogas descriptions, courtesy: New Leaf Paper Eco-Audit, www.newleafpaper.com)

Eco-Logo ~ Before granting its environmental choice™ EcoLogo™ to a product or service, Environment Canada uses life-cycle review to evaluate the environmental impacts of the product or service. (www.ec.gc.ca/ecocycle/issue2/en/p7.cfm)

When you find a certification that is unfamiliar and is not found in our short list, remember our rule: A-S-K! We welcome you to contact one of our friendly resources listed in this guide for a knowledgeable, welcoming, friendly hand. Enjoy the learning process ~ it is as easy as picking up a phone, knocking on a door, and raising your hand to ask "How do I make THAT 'green'?"[TM]

This section is for you to keep your notes right in this guide so everything is kept together when you make your book "green". We have separated these pages by the different topics we have discussed, so you can jot down your information, comments and contact information quickly when you bring the guide with you to the meetings with your publishing and printing teams. Enjoy—and remember to take time to write a note to yourself about how wonderful your "green" book publishing experience is in the space set aside for this in these pages.

Book Consultant and Publisher

Book Consultant and Publisher

Book Manufacturer and Printer

Book Manufacturer and Printer

Cover Designer, Materials and Endpapers

Cover Designer, Materials and Endpapers

Cover Designer, Materials and Endpapers

Cover Designer, Materials and Endpapers

Paper

Paper

_____

_____

_____

_____

_____

_____

_____

_____

Paper

Ink

_____

_____

_____

_____

_____

_____

_____

_____

_____

_____

Eco-Audits

Certifications

_____

_____

_____

_____

_____

_____

_____

_____

_____

Authors Save World™ Program

My "Green" Book Publishing Experience

My "Green" Book Publishing Experience

Other

Other

_____

_____

_____

_____

_____

_____

_____

_____

_____

Other

_____

_____

_____

_____

_____

_____

_____

_____

_____

ABOUT THE AUTHORS

Cindy Katz

A master educator in Science, Mathematics, Writing, Languages, Personal Growth programs, and others, Cindy Katz is a Mother at heart. With five children of her own, she has found ways to communicate seemingly difficult subjects and missions with ease to children of all ages. With Mother Earth as her esteemed colleague and friend, Cindy focuses her energy night and day on educating individuals and businesses around the world about the value of her mission to care for the environment in their every day lives.

With a Masters Degree in Ecology and Zoology from the University of Tel Aviv, Bachelors Degrees of Art in Biology and Education from Rutgers University, and biology, marine science and ecology research experience at the University of Texas and the University of New South Wales in Australia, Cindy has studied the ecological balance in depth between a healthy Mother Earth and the daily activities of companies, families and individuals.

As CEO and Founder of Plant a Tree USA™, Cindy's mission is to plant 18 billion trees and educate millions, creating a healthy Mother Earth with a passion.

As a part of her mission at Plant a Tree USA™, Cindy developed a specific program for authors and publishers called the Authors Save World™ program to promote tree plantings and raise awareness in the publishing industry.

Cindy is dedicated to helping businesses discover opportunities to make their processes and methods of production and delivery ecologically responsible. She also specializes in educating and encouraging businesses to inform their consumers and business-to-business clients about how they save money and make money by being green.

To learn more about Plant a Tree USA™:
www.PlantATreeUSA.com

Cindy has always been interested in uniting industries, organizations and people that seem to compete to be at the forefront of the "green" initiative in their area. In addition to promoting what they've done so far, she has found that by asking the questions that no one is asking results in advancing the "green" efforts of each industry forward in a positive and productive way.

Jennifer S. Wilkov

An international expert in strategic planning and business development for many of the nation's top companies, including American Express and Revlon, and a former Certified Financial Planner, Jennifer S. Wilkov has over a decade of experience with building sustainable businesses and producing high-impact marketing strategies.

She is one of today's sought-after speakers and trainers on how to build businesses through proper planning, effective networking, and sound marketing strategies that work.

LIGHTNING SPEED PRODUCTIONS LLC
www.LightningSpeedProductions.com

She is a best-selling award winning author, publisher, speaker and teacher, freelance writer, entrepreneur, business mentor, humanitarian and philanthropist.

In 12 months, she started 3 sustainable businesses in 3 different industries. She wrote, produced, and published 3 books, including the best-selling award winning book ~ *Dating Your Money*. She published 3 articles in nationwide magazines and has been quoted in newspapers and magazines. She has been interviewed on the top 100 radio stations in the nation and heard by over 11,000,000 listeners. She has also been interviewed on television stations across the nation.

Publishing and Book Consulting:
E.S.P. Press Corp.
www.GetMyESPPress.com

The Green Guide Girls™ Speak!

The Green Guide Girls™ are lively, light, and lovely speakers. Through their "it's easy to be 'green' when you know what to do approach", the Green Guide Girls™ enthusiastically engage audiences and reveal friendly "green" industry information and resources just waiting to be discovered. Through educational, fun and interactive programs, Cindy and Jennifer radiate passion from the platform. The Green Guide Girls™ encourage everyone to ask their famous question, "How do we make THAT 'green'?"™

The presentations are inspirational, as two little girls with pigtails cultivate a collaborative spirit which leads to innovative solutions and transforms industries.

To have the Green Guide Girls™ appear at your next event, please e-mail info@greenguidegirls.com or call the Green Guide Girls™ at 1-646-651-1148.

The Green Guide Girls™ Affiliate Program

Now that you know the secrets to making your books "green"

Share the Wealth!

What if you made more green while showing others how to make their books "green"?

Become an elite affiliate member of the Green Guide Girls™ and help us get the message out that "'Green' is Good for Publishing and the Planet!"

As an author, what if you could make money while writing your books by educating others about how you asked your publishing team, "How do I make THAT book 'green'?"™

Imagine how the publishing world will transform overnight when the publishers, book manufacturers, printers and book consultants you know all have this great information to share with their customers and clients!

It's simple, fun and easy!

Join the Green Guide Girls™ ~ Become an Affiliate member! Please go to www.greenguidegirls.com, click on the Affiliate Program link, and fill out the form online. Raise your hand and benefit by helping others ask, "How do I make THAT book 'green'?"™ And then...

Enjoy sharing the "green" wealth!

www.PlantATreeUSA.com

Plant a Tree USA™ is an ecologically friendly reforestation company.

Join the Authors Save World™ international program to encourage your readers to plant trees and support your favorite charity.
Go to www.AuthorsSaveWorld.com

Involvement with the program ...
• costs nothing to you
• offers you as an author and your book another opportunity to be "green"
• generates funds for you or your favorite charity

See the last page of this book for a visual example of how you as an author can contribute to a "green" book by including the Plant a Tree USA™ Authors Save World™ program. Share this international campaign with your publishing team. We have a full team of farmers, planters, eco-responsible printers, and our wind-powered, carbon-neutral fulfillment center ready to assist authors, publishers, companies, organizations, and individuals to great growth, through tree plantings. Plant a Tree USA™ is planning on planting 18 billion trees, in the USA and internationally.

Plant a Tree USA™'s CEO, Cindy Katz, has been named "Tree Angel", in response to her business to business campaigns. Plant a Tree USA™ is a for-benefit enterprise, combining the best giving, charity, and conservation ideas and actions of a non-profit and the excitement and ability to make progress of the entrepreneurial world.

Contact Plant a Tree USA™ at
trees@plantatreeusa.com or 1-877-A-Tree-4-U

Plant a Tree today.

Go to www.plantatreeusa.com and
Enter Eco-code GREENGUIDEGIRLS

A portion of the tree planting funds go to
The Green Guide Girls Foundation to fund
authors on their "green" quest to make
their books environmentally friendly.

The Green Guide Girls™ encourage tree plantings.
Trees come from paper and paper from trees.
Paper is the material for books.
On each book we sell, we encourage tree plantings
to replenish our Earth with resources.

"We are responsible for our part in planting 18 billion trees."

E.S.P. Press Corp., Jennifer S. Wilkov, and Cindy Katz
are active participants in the Plant a Tree USA™
International "Authors Save World™" campaign.